Computer
Hobbyists
Handbook

FREE CATALOGUE

Computer Hobbyists Handbook

by

R. A. & J. W. Penfold

BERNARD BABANI (publishing) LTD
THE GRAMPIANS
SHEPHERDS BUSH ROAD
LONDON W6 7NF
ENGLAND

PLEASE NOTE

© 1989 BERNARD BABANI (publishing) LTD

First Published — May 1989

British Library Cataloguing in Publication Data
Penfold, R. A.
     Computer hobbyist's handbook
     1. Microcomputer systems
     I. Title   II. Penfold, J. W.
     004.16

ISBN 0 85934 196 8

Printed and Bound by The Guernsey Press Co. Ltd, Channel Islands

Preface

There is a well known computer saying which runs along the lines "there are true standards, broad standards, and computer standards". This may seem rather a pessimistic view of the computer world, but in the past the practical experience of computer users has tended to verify this belief. Changing to a different computer almost invariably meant changing all the software and peripherals as well. About the only equipment that would be likely to operate with the new system was the mains plugs! Fortunately, things have improved considerably over the years, and software compatibility has to some extent arrived. Also, manufacturers' own interfaces have largely disappeared in favour of standard types (albeit with a range of different connectors in most cases).

The aim of this book is to provide a useful range of data and general information on a variety of computer topics, including such things as interfaces, computer languages, MIDI, and numbering systems. There is also a useful lexicon of computer terms, and some helpful appendices. This book is not intended to be a course in computing, but does provide a useful reference for data and information in a single source where it can be quickly and easily found. It does not simply supply raw data, but where necessary detailed explanations are also included. It should be equally useful to both beginners and more experienced hobbyists.

R. A. & J. W. Penfold

ACKNOWLEDGEMENTS

Many of the names and terms mentioned in this book are registered trademarks of various manufacturing, computer, semiconductor and/or software companies. For example:—

ST and ST BASIC are registered trademarks of the Atari Corporation.

IBM, PC, XT, AT, PS/2, PC-DOS and OS/2 are registered trademarks of the International Business Machines Corporation.

GEM, DR LOGO, CP/M, CP/M Plus and DOS PLUS are registered trademarks of Digital Research Incorporated.

BASIC-2, Mallard BASIC and LocoScript are registered trademarks of Locomotive Software Limited.

MS-DOS is a registered trademark of the Microsoft Corporation.

AMSTRAD is a registered trademark of Amstrad Consumer Electronics plc.

Turbo C and Turbo BASIC are registered trademarks of Borland International.

UNIX is a registered trademark of AT & T.

8086, 8088, 80286 and 80386 are registered trademarks of the Intel Corporation.

Z80 is a registered trademark of the Zilog Corporation.

6800 and 68000 are registered trademarks of the Motorola Corporation.

6502 is a registered trademark of the Mostek Corporation.

CONTENTS

Chapter 1

THE POPULAR MICROPROCESSORS

Considering the large number of models of micro-computer which have been produced, the number of microprocessors which have been used is relatively small. Of course, to the majority of users, the actual MPU (microprocessor unit — the usual abbreviation for microprocessor) used is immaterial as the computer will only be programmed in high-level languages, or used with commercial software.

For the enthusiast, however, or for someone who wants to program in assembly language, the MPU used may be a key feature in choosing a machine. The information given here should give an indication of how easy (or otherwise) a particular microprocessor is to program in assembly language.

Here we present details of the major MPUs used in popular computers, plus a few rare ones. These have been somewhat arbitrarily divided into groups, the precursors, 8-bit chips, 16-bit chips, and leading edge designs. For each major chip we give a potted history, details of registers, address modes and comments.

Precursors

The 8080

The Intel 8080 first appeared in 1973. The importance of this chip is not so much in what it achieved itself, but more in the fact that it was the starting point for the later Z80 and 8086/8088 designs — arguably the most important microprocessors in data processing applications.

Another important fact about the 8080 was that the CP/M operating system was originally written for it. This operating system was the first really successful microcomputer operating system, and was dominant in the market in the late '70s and early '80s, and is still very much in use.

The 8080 series have eight 8-bit registers, which can be paired to form four 16-bit registers. Most important of these is the accumulator, which is used as the destination for many arithmetic and logic operations. This register can be paired with the flag register for some operations. Normally the flag register gives information about the result of operations on the accumulator.

The remaining sets of registers are called the BC, DE and HL pairs, names which were carried over to subsequent designs. All these can be used as general purpose data or address registers, but the HL pair is of particular importance as a memory pointer for several memory reference instructions, and also as an accumulator for 16-bit arithmetic.

There are also a 16-bit program counter, and a 16-bit stack pointer. As is usual for 8-bit microprocessors, the 8080 has 8-bit data and 16-bit address buses, allowing 64K of memory to be directly addressed.

One problem with the 8080 was that the specialist nature of some of the registers meant that the programmer had to remember which operations used which register, and that the instruction set was somewhat irregular and messy. Unfortunately this is something else which has been carried over to subsequent designs!

The 8080 has a basic set of 78 instructions, covering arithmetic, logic, and data moving operations, and also conditional and unconditional jumps, I/O operations, and interrupts.

There are four address modes. Direct addressing includes the memory address in the instruction. Register addressing specifies a register or register pair. Register indirect again specifies a register or register pair, but this time containing the address of the data rather than the data itself. Finally, in immediate addressing, the data immediately follows the instruction opcode in memory.

Intel produced an improved version of the 8080, the 8085A, but this found uses mostly in control applications.

The 6800

First appearing in 1974, the Motorola 6800 is another design more important for what followed than for itself. It never achieved any real success in data processing applications, though it was widely used for educational "one board" computers, and in some control applications (they are often to be found in computer printers, for instance).

The main problem with the 6800 was its lack of registers. It had two general purpose 8-bit accumulators, and a 16-bit index register, but that is all. This makes programming for data processing applications difficult.

The register set is typically Motorola, being elegant and straightforward, and this was in large part the reason for the success of the 6800 in tutorial applications. There are 72 basic instructions, but as many are able to use more than one of the address modes, the actual instruction count is 197.

The available address modes are Direct addressing, in which a single byte address is specified in the instruction (so only the bottom 256 bytes, or "zero page", of memory can be accessed); Extended, like direct, but with a two-byte address covering the whole of memory; Immediate, in which the instruction contains the data after the opcode; Inherent, in which the instruction implies the location of the data (i.e. a register); Relative, which allows branching in memory of +129 to −125 bytes relative to the program counter; and Indexed, which adds an offset specified in the instruction to the contents of the index register to form the address of the data.

Later designs which follow on from the 6800 include the MOSTEC 6502, the Motorola 6809, and even the very advanced 68000 series owe their parentage in part to this early design.

The 8-Bit Chips

The 6502

The 6502 is, if you include slight variants such as the 6510, a contender for the title of "most popular chip used in home computers". It is the MPU used in the Apple I, II, and III computers, the 8-bit Ataris, the Commodore Pet and VIC-20, the BBC A, B, and Master series, and (6510) in the Commodore C-64. It has also been used in some less successful models, such as the Acorn Electron and the Oric 1 and Oric Atmos.

The 6502 was developed by MOS Technology from the Motorola 6800, but in an interesting and unusual way. Instead of adding extra features and instructions, the normal course when developing a new design from an existing one, the 6502 had all unnecessary features removed, ending up with very few registers and a small (but adequate) instruction set. There was no attempt to maintain compatibility with the 6800.

It may be thought that this would make the MPU difficult to program, but far from it. There are some difficulties, but on the whole, it is a lovely processor to program in assembly language, and even programming directly in machine code is possible to some extent, something one could not say about most other microprocessors intended for data processing applications.

The lack of registers is partially offset by the fact that the bottom 256 bytes of memory (known as "zero page") can be accessed more rapidly than the

The 6502 is used in a number of home computers. This fast (2 MHz) "A" version is in a BBC model B. The other large chips are display and serial port support chips.

rest of the address range (as the full address can be contained in one byte instead of two) and so zero page is normally reserved and used instead of internal registers for many purposes.

The 6502 is very much an 8-bit chip. All the internal registers are 8-bit, except the address register which has 16 bits, allowing a 64K memory space to be directly addressed. It follows from this that the chip has an 8-bit data bus and a 16-bit address bus.

The 6502 does seem to be very lacking in registers, having only an accumulator and two index registers, X and Y. The accumulator has to be used as the destination in arithmetic and logical operations. The X and Y registers are intended mainly for use as indexes to addresses, but can be used as general-purpose registers. With some exceptions, they can be used interchangeably.

The stack pointer is also only 8 bits, restricting stack size to 256 bytes. Since a major use of the stack is to save the contents of the registers during subroutine calls, with only 8-bit registers a 256-byte stack is not too much of a problem. The stack always occupies "page 1" of memory (0100 to 01FF hex). The 8-bit size of the index registers is not too much of a problem as they are normally used to access small blocks of data of less than 256 bytes. Handling larger blocks of memory than this does require some extra programming.

In fact, the 6502 treats the whole of memory as if it were organised into 256 byte "pages", and any operation on memory which must work across a page boundary involves extra work.

All of this does not, however, mean that the 6502 is a slow processor. The simplicity of the instruction set allows fast decoding, and the processor also uses "pipelining", where the next instruction is decoded while the current one is still executing. This gives the 6502 a very fast read-modify-write cycle.

For I/O operations, the 6502 uses a memory-mapped system, thus dispensing with the need for specific input and output instructions. This does mean, however, that peripheral chips appear in the memory map, taking up some of the available address range. The 6502 has just two levels of interrupts, maskable and non-maskable. 6502-based computers usually use some form of polling system to service interrupts.

One very useful feature of the 6502 in some applications is its ability to perform BCD (binary coded decimal) arithmetic directly. Once a special bit in the flags register has been set, all arithmetic will be performed in BCD until the flag is cleared.

The 6502 has just 56 instructions in the instruction set, but a claimed 13 addressing modes, which allow the limited instruction set to be used to best advantage.

1. ACCUMULATOR ADDRESSING. This mode is used by instructions which operate on the 6502's accumulator without requiring external data. Such operations may, however, require some external memory access, i.e. the stack, or also involve the X or Y registers.

2. IMPLIED ADDRESSING. This mode of addressing is used only by instructions which operate on one or more of the 6502's internal registers without requiring external data. Such operations may, however, require some external memory access, e.g. the stack.

3. IMMEDIATE ADDRESSING. In this mode, the operand is included in the program, immediately after the opcode for the instruction.

4. ABSOLUTE ADDRESSING. In absolute addressing the location of the operand in memory is specified in the instruction, in two bytes immediately following the opcode.

5. ZERO PAGE. This is a special form of absolute addressing where the opcode is followed by a single-byte address. This is used as the low byte of a 2-byte address, the high byte being assumed to be zero, thus only the zero page of memory can be accessed. This mode of addressing has a speed advantage over normal absolute addressing.

6. RELATIVE ADDRESSING. With the 6502, this address mode is only available for branch instructions. The byte following the opcode is regarded as a signed displacement, from −128 to +127. If the program branches as a result of the branch instruction (i.e. if the test is true) this displacement is added to the program counter, causing a backward or forward jump. (With most assemblers, you specify an address to which the program is to branch, and the assembler calculates the displacement for you.)

7. INDIRECT ADDRESSING. In indirect addressing, two bytes following the opcode contain a memory address. The contents of this address, and the byte following it, give a further address, which is where the data is to be found. True indirect addressing is extremely rare in microprocessors, and the 6502 allows it only for a single instruction, JMP.

8. INDEXED ABSOLUTE X ADDRESSING. In this mode, the instruction contains a two-byte address to which the contents of the X-index register is added. As the index registers can be easily incremented and decremented, this mode allows easy manipulation of blocks of memory of 256 bytes or less.

9. INDEXED ABSOLUTE Y ADDRESSING. This is the same as 8, except for using the Y register instead of the X.

10. INDEXED ZERO PAGE X ADDRESSING. The byte following the opcode in this mode contains an address in zero page to which the contents of the X

register is added. However, no page boundary crossing is allowed so if the result exceeds 00FF hex, a wrap-around in page zero occurs.

11. INDEXED ZERO PAGE Y ADDRESSING. The same as 10, except that it can only be used with two instructions concerned with loading and saving the X register.

12. INDEXED INDIRECT ADDRESSING. This mode uses the X-index register. The contents of this register is added to the contents of a single byte in the instruction, to form an address in zero page (no page boundary crossing allowed, as for 9 and 10 above). The contents of the byte pointed to and the next byte form the effective address for the instruction. In effect, this instruction allows zero page to be treated as a set of 16-bit address registers.

13. INDIRECT INDEXED ADDRESSING. This mode uses the Y-index register. A byte in the instruction is regarded as an address in zero page, and the contents of this address and the byte following it have the contents of the Y register added to them to form the effective address for the instruction. This mode can be used to manipulate blocks of memory of more than 265 bytes, but the high byte of the address in zero page is not incremented or decremented automatically when required, so code must be written to do this.

The 6502 family includes a number of other MPUs such as the 6503, which has a 4K address range and comes in a 28-pin package (the 6505 and 6506 are similar but with control line differences), and the 6504, which has an 8K address range and also comes in a 28-pin package (the 6507 is similar but with RDY instead of IRQ). The 6512 is a special version intended for dual-processor applications. The 6513 and 6515 are also intended for dual-processor applications, have a 4K address range and come in 28-pin packages. The 65C02 is a low-power CMOS technology version of the basic 6502, and the 65C102 is similar, but with some extra instructions added (mostly made up of combinations of original instructions), intended to simplify programming of interrupt servicing and subroutine calls.

One of the most important things about the 6502 is that it is widely regarded as one of the precursors of the so-called RISC (Reduced Instruction Set Chip) chips, which are becoming an increasingly important strand of microprocessor design.

The Z80
Just as the 6502 was developed from the 6800, so the Z80 was developed by Zilog from the Intel 8080 design. However, the Z80 designers took the much more obvious path of adding features and instructions, while maintaining compatibility with the earlier chip. The result of this is that the Z80 is undeniably

powerful, and with a comprehensive instruction set, but it is not exactly an elegant design! The instruction set is rather untidy, and there are many restrictions on which instructions can use which address modes, so that few programmers would try to write Z80 assembly language without the manual open at their side.

In terms of the number of models of computer designed around the chip, the Z80 can easily claim the title of "most popular microprocessor". In the field of home computers, the Z80 is best known as the heart of the immensely popular Sinclair ZX Spectrum models, and it was also used in the earlier ZX80 and ZX81. It is also used in the hardly less popular Amstrad CPC series, and in other models too numerous to list.

The decision to maintain compatibility with the 8080 was a good move on the part of Zilog, as it meant the Z80 had a good software base available when introduced, including most importantly, the Digital Research CP/M operating system. This O.S. was very widely used during the early '80's (and still is), and in fact there were far more Z80 based CP/M systems designed than 8080 based, to the extent that many people nowadays believe that CP/M was in fact developed for the Z80.

By the standards of 8-bit microprocessors, the Z80 has a very large set of general purpose registers. In fact, there are two complete sets of 4 sixteen-bit registers, with two instructions to switch between them. This is very useful when servicing interrupts, as it allows the registers to be "saved" by switching to the alternate set, instead of stacking them. These 16-bit registers can also be used as pairs of 8-bit registers.

The program counter has sixteen bits, as does the single stack pointer. The Z80 also has two sixteen-bit index registers. There are also two registers which are peculiar to the Z80. The I register is used during a special interrupt mechanism called Mode 3, and the R register is used for memory refresh purposes.

The Z80 has an 8-bit data bus and a 16-bit address bus, allowing it to directly access 64K of memory. It has special I/O instructions, so peripherals do not use up space in the memory map.

The instruction set comprises some 158 instructions. This compares with 78 on the 8080. Though there is compatibility between the two chips at the source code level, some of the assembly language mnemonics have been changed for the Z80.

Zilog claim 10 addressing modes for the Z80, though it is hard to see how they arrive at this figure. Manufacturers all have their own ideas as to what constitutes an addressing mode. The following is a summary of the modes available, and is comprehensive, though it does not follow the manufacturer's ideas exactly.

1. IMPLIED ADDRESSING. This is used by those instructions which operate on one or more of the

The Z80 is available under other type numbers. This NEC version is in a ZX81.

Z80's registers without requiring external data. (Zilog make a distinction between implied addressing, which is limited to instructions which do not have a specific field to point to an internal register, and register addressing for instructions which do.)

2. IMMEDIATE ADDRESSING. In this mode, the operand is included in the instruction immediately after the opcode. As the Z80 has both 8-bit and 16-bit registers, there are two types of immediate addressing, for 8-bit and 16-bit operands. Where the operand is 16 bits long, the mode is sometimes called immediate extended.

3. ABSOLUTE ADDRESSING. In absolute addressing, the location of the operand in memory is specified in the instruction. The address is two bytes long, so anywhere in the 64K of memory possible can be accessed.

4. ABSOLUTE SHORT ADDRESSING. Similar to 3, but the address occupies only a single byte, so only addresses in the first 256 bytes of memory can be

accessed (similar to the 6502's zero page). This mode is only used by the RST instruction.

5. RELATIVE ADDRESSING. In this mode, the byte following the opcode is regarded as a displacement from +127 to −128. This is added to the program counter to cause a program branch. Only used by JR (jump relative) instructions. With most assemblers, you would specify the address to which you wish the program to branch, and the assembler will calculate the displacement for you.

6. REGISTER INDIRECT ADDRESSING. Here, any of the register pairs BC, DE or HL may be used to contain the address where the operand is to be found. Where the registers are used to point to two-byte data, the low byte is at the address specified, and the high byte at the next higher address in memory.

7. INDEXED ADDRESSING. In indexed addressing, the address specified in the instruction is modified by having added to it the contents of either the IX or IY

5

index register, thus giving the effective address for the instruction. This is mostly used for accessing elements in tables of data.

Zilog followed up the Z80 with the Z8000 (16-bit) and Z800 (8-16 bit with Z80 compatibility), but neither of these has achieved any real success.

The 6809

Like the 6502, the 6809 was developed, in a sense, from the 6800/6802, but this time by Motorola themselves. They took a different course from either MOS Technology with the 6502, or Zilog with the Z80 (from the 8080). The 6809 was largely a new design, without extra registers untidily tacked on or a messy instruction set, but a degree of code compatibility with the 6800 at the source code (assembly language) level was maintained.

The 6809 is a very elegant design, with a nice tidy set of registers, and an easy-to-use instruction set devoid of complications as to which instructions can use which address modes. It is, in the opinion of many, the best of the 8-bit chips.

It is therefore unfortunate to have to record that the 6809 has never been used in a computer worthy of its talents. The only notable designs to employ it have been the Dragon and the Tandy Colour Computer, which in fact are very similar machines in terms of electronics. Though not bad computers, they were never among the best. The problem for the 6809 was that it came along too late, when programmers had learned to live with the deficiencies (real and imagined) of the Z80 and 6502, and these chips had acquired considerable software bases.

The 6809 has two 8-bit accumulators, which can be used together as a single 16-bit register. It also has two 16-bit index registers, and two 16-bit stack pointers. The ability to maintain two independent stacks makes it easy to implement high-level languages. The 6809 has a form of zero-page, allowing a 256-byte page in memory to be used, in effect, as extra data registers, but thanks to an 8-bit direct page register, this can be anywhere in the memory map.

The data bus is 8 bits wide, and the address bus 16 bits, allowing 64K of memory to be directly addressed. Memory mapped I/O is used.

There is a basic set of 59 mnemonics in 6809 assembly language, but with variations allowed, and ten address modes available, there are in effect some 1464 instructions available. So elegant and straightforward is the 6809 instruction set that it is the favourite of many programmers for assembly language programming. Uniquely in 8-bit microprocessors, the 6809 has an 8-bit multiply instruction, yielding a 16 bit result. This gives some idea of the advanced nature of the design.

The claim of 10 addressing modes for the 6809 is an honest one. As some other manufacturers count, there could be as many as 20.

1. INHERENT ADDRESSING. Like implied addressing, where the instruction implies any necessary addressing information.

2. IMMEDIATE ADDRESSING. The data for the instruction comes immediately after the opcode in memory, and can be one or two bytes long.

3. EXTENDED ADDRESSING. In this mode, the 16-bit address of the data follows the opcode in memory.

4. EXTENDED INDIRECT ADDRESSING. One of the very few examples of true indirection in microprocessors. In this mode, the two bytes after the opcode contain the address in memory where the *address* of the data is to be found.

5. DIRECT ADDRESSING. This is similar to the 6502's zero page addressing. Where the opcode is followed by an 8-bit address. However, the high byte of the address, instead of being forced to be zero, is obtained from the direct page register, so any page in memory can be used.

6. REGISTER ADDRESSING. In this mode the opcode is followed by a reference to one or more of the registers to be used in the operation.

7. INDEXED ADDRESSING. Really a whole range of register-indirect addressing modes which can use either of the index registers, either of the stack pointers, and in some cases the program counter. In general the contents of a register are added to an offset, which can be *zero offset*, self-explanatory; *constant offset*, where the offset is a two's complement number 5, 8, or 16 bits in length following the opcode; *accumulator offset*, which uses an 8 or 16 bit offset stored in one of or both of the accumulators; *auto increment*, where a zero offset is used and the pointer register is incremented by one or two after it has been used, allowing tables of one or two byte data to be stepped through automatically; and finally *auto decrement*, allowing tables to be stepped through backwards.

8. INDIRECT INDEXED ADDRESSING. Used *in addition* to one of the previous modes. In this case, the address formed by the indexed mode points to the *address of* the data, not the data itself.

9. RELATIVE ADDRESSING. This mode allows jumping forward or backward in memory relative to the program counter. A 16-bit offset is allowed, so the whole of memory can be covered. This mode is used only by branch instructions.

10. PROGRAM COUNTER RELATIVE ADDRESSING. This mode allows data to be accessed not by an absolute address, but by their current difference from

the program counter. This mode, together with the previous one, allows the writing of position independent code, a very useful feature.

Though the 6809 never achieved great commercial success, at least as far as use in home micros is concerned, it was the immediate precursor of the Motorola 68000 series of 8/16, 16 and 32 bit micro-processors, widely regarded as the finest MPUs currently available, at least as far as Comprehensive Instruction Set Chips (CISC) are concerned.

The 1802

The 1802 MPU from RCA is one of the less well known devices, but has probably been used to a greater extent than many in the computer world would think. It was in fact used in a home computer called the "Comx 35", but this never sold in any numbers in the U.K. By most accounts it was quite fast for an 8 bit machine, which would suggest that the 1802 does not lack anything in performance if used skillfully. The 1802's claim to fame is that it is a CMOS device, which means that it achieves a low level of power consumption. These days a number of popular MPUs are available in low power CMOS versions, which has severely reduced the popularity of the 1802. However, it was first launched quite early in MPU history (about 1973), and at that time it was the only low power microprocessor that was avail-able. In fact it remained the only low power micro-processor for a number of years. It achieved substantial sales, probably because it could be used in battery powered control systems etc. where the high current consumption of other MPUs made them virtually unusable.

The 1802 is rather crude by modern standards, although it has one or two advanced features such as built-in clock generator and DMA (direct memory access) controller. It has sixteen 16-bit general purpose registers, and its instruction set very much revolves around these. They can be used as program counters, data registers, or memory pointers. The 1802 tends to be a little confusing when first using the device, but it can work well in control applica-tions. It can also run interpreted languages surprisingly fast (as in the Comx 35 with its inter-preted BASIC). It seems likely though, that the 1802 will continue to give way to low power versions of more recent devices.

The 16-Bit Chips

The TI9900

The 9900 was introduced in 1976, and thus has some claim to be the first 16-bit chip. It was, however, fabricated using the technology of the 8-bit chips, and this lead to some idiosyncracies in the design. The memory address range was also limited to that which would be expected of an 8-bit chip.

The only computer to employ this chip was Texas Instruments' own TI99. This computer had its good points, but was very expensive and enjoyed only a limited success, largely as a home games machine. It now has a small cult following. The chip itself achieved success in other fields, such as in navigation systems and avionics where the 16-bit architecture was a real benefit.

It follows from this that the 9900 has never acquired a large general-purpose software base.

One feature of the 9900, largely dictated by the use of 1976 technology, is that there are very few registers indeed on the chip itself. Most of them, including even the accumulator, are in RAM. The only registers on-chip are a 15-bit program counter (to address 32K *words* of memory — byte addressing not being possible), the status register, and a *work-space pointer*. This is used to point to the area of RAM which is being used as the registers which would normally be on the chip. There are effectively 16 registers in a workspace, 6 of which have (at least in part) dedicated functions. The remainder are general purpose in nature. Multiple workspaces are possible, so interrupts can be handled by switching workspaces rather than by saving the registers on the stack.

As already mentioned, the address bus is 15 bits wide, and the data bus is 16 bits, as one would expect from a true 16-bit chip.

The 9900 instruction set contains 72 basic instruc-, tions, so is quite easy to learn, but coupled with eight address modes (of which some instructions can use 5, others one of the remaining 3) it is also quite flexible and comprehensive.

As you might expect, many of the eight address modes are unique to the 9900.

1. WORKSPACE REGISTER ADDRESSING. This is similar to implied or inherent addressing modes, where the instruction contains the address of the workspace register which contains the operand.

2. WORKSPACE REGISTER INDIRECT ADDRESSING. Here, the opcode includes the address of a register which contains the *address* of the data.

3. WORKSPACE REGISTER INDIRECT AUTO INCREMENT ADDRESSING. This is the same as (2), except that after the data has been fetched, the register is incremented. This instruction is used for stepping through tables of (16-bit) data.

4. SYMBOLIC ADDRESSING. This is really direct addressing, in which the address of the data follows the opcode in program memory.

5. INDEXED ADDRESSING. In this mode, a base address follows the opcode in memory, and the contents of a register is added to this to form the

effective address. The contents of the register is a signed number, allowing positive or negative offsets from the base.

6. IMMEDIATE ADDRESSING. Conventional, where the word of memory immediately after the instruction contains the operand.

7. PROGRAM COUNTER RELATIVE ADDRESSING. Used only for jump instructions, and has a range of −128 to +127 *words.*

8. CRU RELATIVE ADDRESSING. This mode is used for I/O operations. The 9900 has a unique Communications Register Unit for I/O.

The 8086 Series

When Intel saw the success which Zilog had with the Z80, essentially an improved 8080A, they decided not to respond with an enhanced 8080 design of their own, but instead to move on directly to the next generation of 16-bit chips. Thus the 8086, which was one of the first true sixteen-bitters to become commercially available. The 8086 was an almost immediate success, both in data processing and in control applications.

The 8086 was quickly followed by the 8088, a software-compatible design but with an 8-bit data bus. This MPU has full 16-bit architecture inside but is slower in operation as it requires two fetches for word-length data. It has the advantage of allowing cheaper systems to be constructed around it.

In fact, the 8088 was for a long time the more successful of the two types, being used in the IBM PC, and many of the compatibles which have been produced in vast numbers. However, the 8086 is now used in the AMSTRAD PC1512/1640 computers, and the sales figures of these could reverse this.

The 8086 series has a vast software support, largely because of its use in the IBM PC. There are two largely compatible operating systems, PC-DOS (IBM) and MS-DOS (Microsoft). Virtually any type of software ever written is available to run under these, including a very wide range of languages.

The 8086 has fourteen 16-bit registers. These are arranged as three sets of four registers, the instruction pointer (program counter) and the flags register.

The set of general purpose registers can be used as either four 16-bit registers or eight 8-bit registers. The registers are essentially similar to those in the 8080A, though the names used are slightly different. Unlike the 8080A, the registers are in general interchangeable rather than dedicated to specific tasks, but there are still some instructions which can only use particular registers.

The second set of registers are called the segment register file and are used for address generation. The 8086 has a unique form of memory management

called segment addressing. The chip can address 1 megabyte of memory, which would require a 20-bit address, but only 16-bit values are handled within the chip. To provide the required 20-bit address, the contents of a segment register is shifted left by four bits, and ANDed with another 16-bit value which may come from the program counter, stack pointer, an index register, a general register, or memory. The four registers allow 64K of memory each, or 256K in all, to be addressed without reloading the registers. The registers are called the Code Segment (CS), Data Segment (DS), Stack Segment (SS), and Extra Segment (ES).

The third set of registers contains index registers and memory pointers. These include the stack pointer (SP), Base Pointer (BP), also used for the stack segment, and the Source Index (SI) and Destination Index (DI) pointers.

The 8086 has a 16-bit data bus and a 20-bit address bus. Multiplexing is used to allow these to be provided in a package with only 40 pins. The 8088 has only an 8-bit data bus.

The 8086 uses the system of having relatively few mnemonics in the instruction set, but modifying these by address mode and other qualifiers to provide a comprehensive range of instructions. There are roughly 100 mnemonics in the instruction set.

There are nine address modes available, the first four of which are conventional. These are:—

REGISTER
IMMEDIATE
DIRECT
REGISTER INDIRECT

The other modes are:—

BASED ADDRESSING. In this mode the effective address is computed by summing a displacement in the instruction with the contents of the BX or BP register. Using the BP register allows access to data on the stack without POPing.

INDEXED ADDRESSING. Here the effective address is computed by summing a displacement with the contents of the SI or DI registers. Normally the displacement will be the base of a table of data, and the index register will be used to step through it.

BASED INDEXED ADDRESSING. The effective address is computed by summing the contents of a base register, an index register and a displacement. The use of two registers allows two-dimensional arrays of data to be accessed.

STRING ADDRESSING. This is used with string instructions which cannot use the above modes. In this mode the index registers are used in place of the SI and DI registers.

I/O DIRECT ADDRESSING. This uses an 8-bit address to directly access one of 256 I/O ports directly.

The Motorola 68000

After the lack of success of the 6800 and 6809 in data processing applications, Motorola countered the Intel design with a processor which did much to consolidate Motorola's reputation for producing designs with both power and elegance.

The 68000 series are 'clean sheet' designs with no attempt at compatibility with previous products. They have, in fact, a 32-bit internal architecture, and various models are available with from 8 to 32-bit data buses, and 20 to 32-bit address buses.

The 68000 series were slower to achieve commercial success than the 8086 series, but are now used in a wide range of computers, including the Apple Macintosh (and the previous Lisa model), the Atari ST series, and the Commodore Amigas. The cutdown 68008 was used (some would say misused) in the ill-fated Sinclair QL, and there are also several very large multi-user systems based on these chips. There are several operating systems implemented from these microprocessors, including versions of UNIX and XENIX for multi-user and multi-tasking applications.

The 68000 series are particularly well endowed with registers. There are eight 32-bit data registers, which are general-purpose in nature and interchangeable (i.e. no instructions have to use a particular register), and seven 32-bit address registers, which can be used as base or index registers, or as extra stack pointers. The address registers can also be used interchangeably. There are also two stack pointers, one for 'user' mode and one for 'supervisor' mode (used for servicing interrupts, among other things), the program counter, and the flags register.

The 68000 has a 16-bit data bus and a 24-bit address bus, thus having an address range of 16 Mbytes. The 68008 has an 8-bit data bus and a 20-bit address bus (1 Mbyte). The 68010 is like the 68000 but with internal support for virtual memory management. The 68020 has the full 32-bit data bus and 32-bit address bus for a 4096 Mbyte address range (!).

The 68000 has a straightforward instruction set with just 56 basic mnemonics, but when multiplied by the available addressing modes and data type options you end up with a set of over 1000 unique

The 68000 micro. This one is fitted in a development system, but this processor is used in popular computers such as the Atari STs and Commodore Amigas.

The 68008 is the 8 bit bus version of the 68000. This device is in a Sinclair QL. Most other computers seem to use the standard 16 bit bus version.

instructions. Most instructions can access byte, word (16-bit) or long word (32bit) data, but only word and long word access can be used with the address registers. Of particular interest is the **MOVE** instruction, which replaces the load and save instructions of other processors, and allows memory to register, register to register, and register to memory data moves, and also direct memory to memory moves *without* using processor registers.

There are fourteen address modes.

1. DATA REGISTER DIRECT. The operand is in a specified data register.

2. ADDRESS REGISTER DIRECT. The operand is in a specified address register.

3. ADDRESS REGISTER INDIRECT. The address of the data is contained in one of the address registers.

4. ADDRESS REGISTER INDIRECT WITH POST INCREMENT. This is similar to (3), but the address

in the register is automatically incremented after use. This can be used for stepping through data tables. The amount of the increment can be 1, 2, or 4 for byte, word or long word data.

5. ADDRESS REGISTER INDIRECT WITH PRE DECREMENT. This is the complement to (4), and is used for stepping *down* through tables. Note that the decrement occurs *before* the data is accessed. These instructions can be used together for stack-type pop and push operations.

6. ADDRESS REGISTER INDIRECT WITH DISPLACEMENT. In this mode, a 16-bit displacement in the instruction is added to the contents of an address register to form the effective address of the data. It is a form of indexed addressing.

7. ADDRESS REGISTER INDIRECT WITH INDEX. This is another form of indexed addressing, but here the index value comes from a data register, and there is also an 8-bit displacement in the instruction. The displacement, contents of the address register and contents of the data register are added together to form the effective address.

8. ABSOLUTE SHORT ADDRESSING. This is a direct addressing mode, but the address can be only 16 bits long. It is similar to 6800 direct or 6502 zero-page addressing, but can access 64K bytes of memory.

9. ABSOLUTE LONG ADDRESSING. A direct addressing mode using a full 32-bit address, capable of accessing any valid memory location.

10. PROGRAM COUNTER RELATIVE WITH DISPLACEMENT. This mode is provided to allow some degree of position-independent code to be written. A 16-bit displacement is added to the contents of the program counter to form the effective address of the data.

11. PROGRAM COUNTER RELATIVE WITH INDEX. In this mode the effective address is formed by adding the contents of the program counter, an index register, and an 8-bit displacement in the instruction. It allows the whole of memory to be accessed relative to the program counter.

12. IMMEDIATE. This mode is conventional, except that (as usual on the 68000) the data may be byte, word, or long word in length.

13. CONDITION CODE/STATUS REGISTER. This mode allows access to the SR or CCR to test, set or reset bits in these registers, using logical instructions.

14. IMPLICIT. This mode is conventional.

Other 16-Bit Designs

The 8086 series and the 68000 series are the only two sixteen bit designs which have achieved commercial success, at least in home and business computers. There are, however, several other designs which have not found wide application but are mentioned here for completeness.

The Zilog Z8000/Z800
The Z8000 appeared shortly after the 8086, and on the face of it seemed to be a better design, having eight times the address range and faster performance. However, sales never really took off. There are many possible reasons for this. The Z8000 was not compatible with any previous product in any degree, but the opportunity of starting with a clean sheet was not used to provide a particularly tidy instruction set. Also, the Z8000 was followed quickly by the 68000, which caught the imagination of designers. The 8086 quickly generated a software base, the 68000 was perceived as the most exciting design, so the Z8000 rather fell between two stools.

In fact, there is no processor actually called the Z8000. This is the generic name for the family of devices, of which there are four. The Z8001 has a 16-bit data bus and a segmented address range of 8 megabytes. The Z8002 comes in a smaller (40 pin instead of 48) package and has a 64K byte address range only. The Z8003 and Z8004 have virtual memory and multi-processor support, but are otherwise identical to the Z8001 and Z8002 respectively.

The Z8000 has a set of 110 basic mnemonics which, in combination with the available data types and address modes expands to a little over 400 discrete instructions. It can be seen that this does not compare well with the 68000 which achieves over 1000 instructions using just 56 mnemonics. There are 8 fairly conventional address modes.

Zilog tried for a second bite at the cherry with the Z800. This is a 16-bit design which is code-compatible with the Z80 8-bit chip, and so can (at least in theory) use the Z80 software base, including CP/M. However, by the time this chip appeared, the 8086 and the MS-DOS/PC-DOS operating systems had become the new industry standard, and all the companies which had formerly produced CP/M machines had moved on to producing IBM PC compatibles. Thus, when this chip arrived, there was simply no place for it in the market.

The Z800 register set is virtually identical to that of the Z80, with the addition of an extra stack pointer. The instruction set is that of the Z80 with all its shortcomings, with the addition of some more "modern" instructions such as multiply and divide. There are nine address modes, many of which obviously are based on those of the Z80, but among the extra ones are Program Counter Relative and Stack Pointer Relative, which give a limited ability for position independent code.

The National Semiconductors 16032 Series
Though National Semiconductors is one of the largest semiconductor manufacturers in the world, they were rather late onto the microprocessor scene. The ambitious 16032 series of designs were intended to enable them to catch up with the leaders.

As with the 68000 series, the 16032 series is a range of compatible designs with 32-bit internal architecture, but with a choice of 8, 16 or 32-bit data bus widths. The designs, in fact, have a great similarity to the Motorola architecture, with eight general-purpose registers and eight special-purpose registers. The instruction set, again like the 68000 series, is also regular and elegant. There are around 100 basic mnemonics, but with 9 address modes and three data types they expand to nearly 1000 distinct instructions.

All the 16032 series support virtual memory operations. The 16032 has a 16-bit data bus and a 24-bit address bus, addressing 16 megabytes of unsegmented memory. The 16008 has a cut-down 8-bit external data bus, but the same address range. The 32032 has full 32-bit data and address buses.

The main problem with the National Semiconductor designs was that they took a long time to actually arrive in volume, and by the time they did, the 68000 series had taken residence in most of the sockets they might have occupied. Such applications as they have found are mostly in the scientific field. The 16032 is available as a second processor for the BBC Micros and is used in the BBC Master Scientific.

The Way Forward

Though the successful 16-bit chips have a long life ahead of them yet, rivals are appearing on the scene. As mentioned in the section on the 6502, there are two schools of thought in microprocessor design. Chips such as the 68000 come from the CISC (Complex [or Comprehensive] Instruction Set Chip) school. The other school favours Reduced Instruction Set Chips (RISC), in which the instruction set is reduced to a relatively few frequently-executed instructions.

The idea behind this is that the microprocessor spends a very high percentage of its time executing these popular instructions, and the remaining instructions are used very infrequently. By reducing the size of the instruction set, the processor has to do less work internally to decode and execute the instructions, thus executing code faster. The jobs done by the omitted instructions can be done by combinations of the remaining instructions when required. Two processors of this type are now available and coming into use, and others are under development, though they may not find their way into home/business computers.

The Acorn ARM

The Acorn ARM comes from the manufacturers of the BBC micros, who wanted a "super 6502" design for a new range of machines. In fact, the ARM (Acorn RISC Machine) is rather more than that. It is used in the Acorn Archimedes computers, which at time of writing are generally accepted as the fastest available microcomputers.

The ARM has 44 instruction codes, to perform such jobs as load/store single registers, load/store multiple registers, arithmetic, logical, branch and software interrupts. Instructions such as multiply and divide, or block moves, are not included. An interesting feature is that all instructions include a conditional test. This helps reduce the number of branches in a program, which would otherwise

reduce the efficiency of the ARM, which uses pipelining to speed up program execution. Each time there is a branch, the already-decoded instructions in the pipeline have to be discarded.

Only two addressing modes are used, base relative and program counter relative. However, the way these are implemented is highly flexible, and allows the more complex modes of CISC chips (such as auto-increment/decrement modes) to be simulated.

The ARM has a 32-bit data bus and a 26-bit address bus, allowing 64 megabytes of memory to be directly addressed. There are 25 32-bit registers on the chip, of which 16 are normally available to the programmer.

At time of writing it is too soon to say how successful the ARM chip and the Archimedes computers will be, but they have the advantage of being able to run both MS-DOS and 6502 software by means of emulators, and they are now beginning to attract native software support.

The INMOS Transputer

The Transputer is a much more radical design than the ARM, being intended as a device for use in arrays to produce parallel-processing machines — a very radical concept.

The basic Transputer is a 32-bit device with 32 bit registers, 32 bit data bus and 32 bit address bus, capable of addressing 4 gigabytes of memory. 16 bit variants are also planned. The chip also has 2K of on-chip memory. Each Transputer also has four high-speed serial data links to other Transputers to enable them to be connected in parallel processing applications.

The Transputer has very few registers, in fact only six, and three of these are dedicated to use as an expression-evaulator stack. The on-chip RAM is used to hold data in place of general-purpose registers.

The Transputer has around 60 instructions in its instruction set, but it is not intended ever to be programmed directly in assembly language. Instead, a special high level language called Occam has been developed for it, and this language is also designed for parallel processing. Addressing modes in the conventional sense do not apply to the Transputer.

Transputer add-on boards are now available for several computers, including the IBM PC and compatibles, and it is the heart of the Atari ABAQ.

Register Diagrams

For handy reference purposes, register set diagrams for the popular 6502, Z80, 68000, and 8086 MPUs are provided in Figures 1.1 to 1.4.

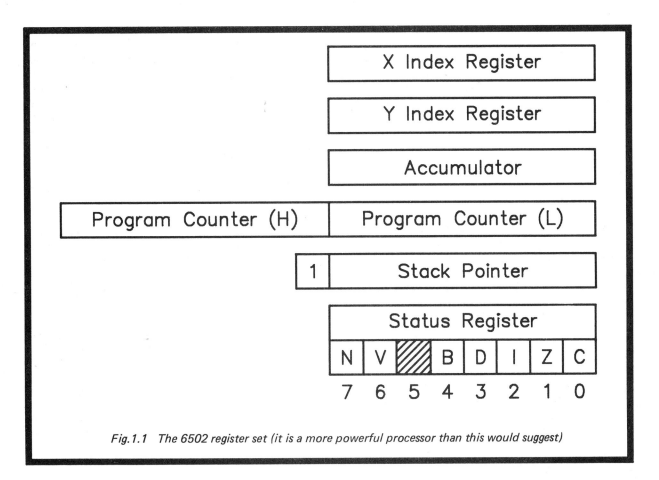

Fig.1.1   The 6502 register set (it is a more powerful processor than this would suggest)

Main Register Set

Accumulator	Flags F
B Register	C Register
D Register	E Register
H Register	L Register

Alternate Register Set

Accumulator'	Flags F'
B Register'	C Register'
D Register'	E Register'
H Register'	L Register'

General Registers

Interrupt Vector I	Refresh R
Index Register X	
Index Register Y	
Stack Pointer	
Program Counter	

Flag Register Details

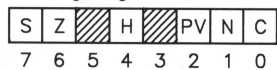

S	Z	░	H	░	PV	N	C
7	6	5	4	3	2	1	0

Fig.1.2 The Z80 register set

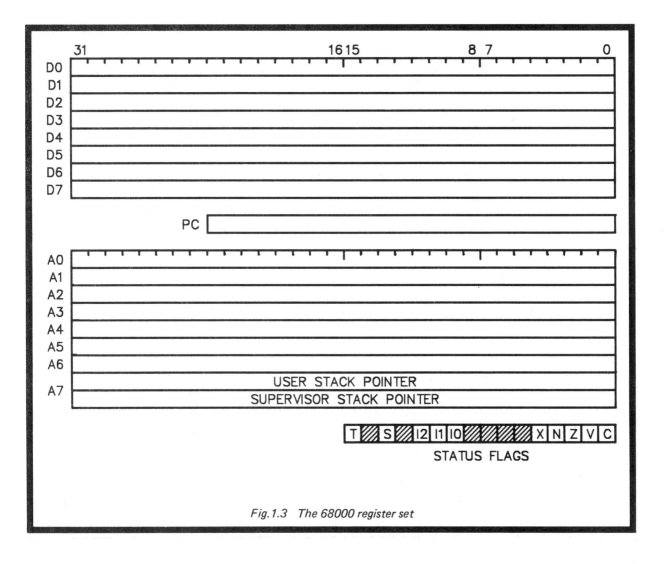

Fig.1.3   The 68000 register set

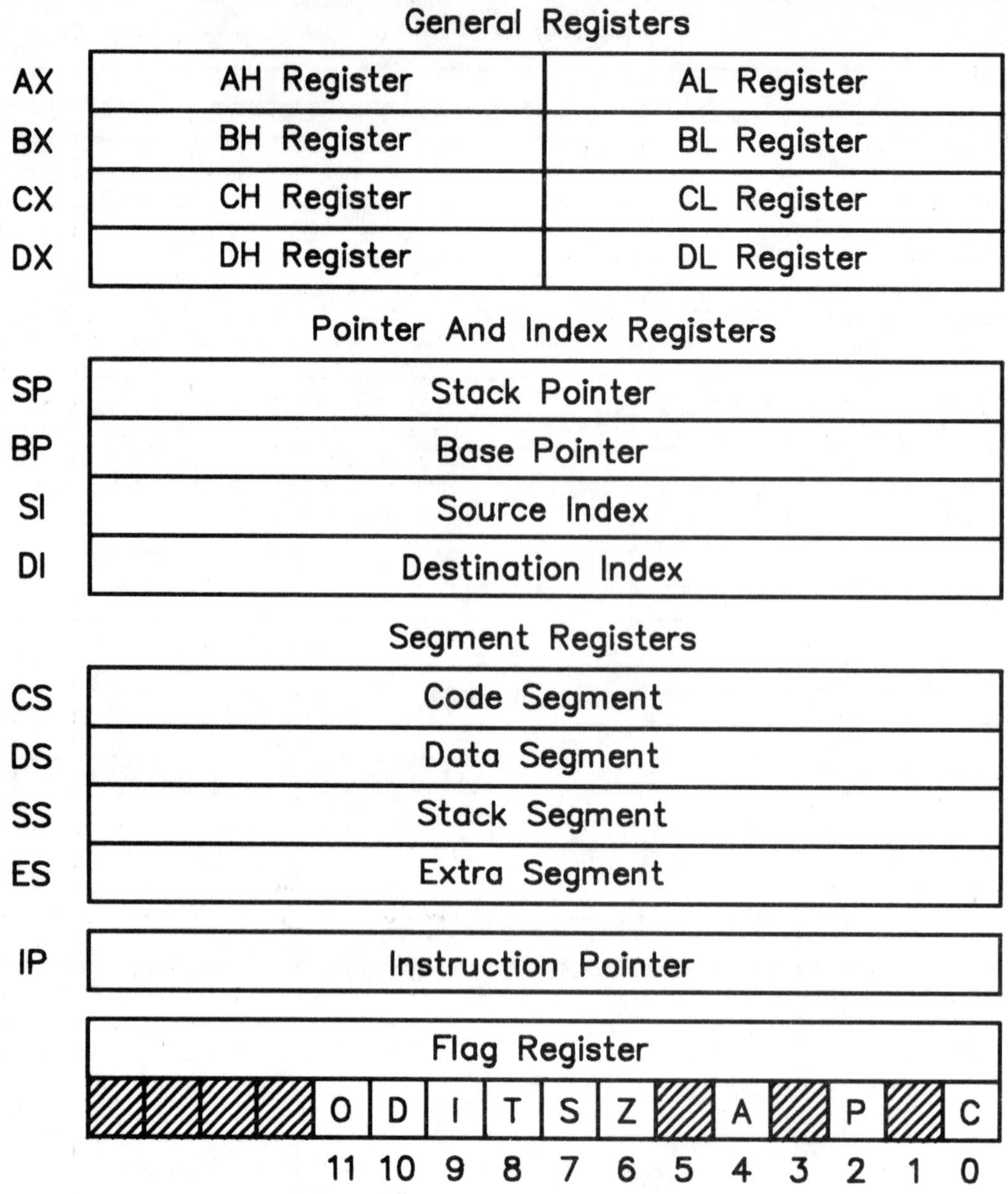

General Registers

AX	AH Register	AL Register
BX	BH Register	BL Register
CX	CH Register	CL Register
DX	DH Register	DL Register

Pointer And Index Registers

SP	Stack Pointer
BP	Base Pointer
SI	Source Index
DI	Destination Index

Segment Registers

CS	Code Segment
DS	Data Segment
SS	Stack Segment
ES	Extra Segment

IP	Instruction Pointer

Flag Register

				O	D	I	T	S	Z		A		P		C
				11	10	9	8	7	6	5	4	3	2	1	0

Fig.1.4   The 8086 register set

Chapter 2

INTERFACES

There can be relatively few people who use a computer system that consists of a single stand-alone unit. The vast majority of computer systems consist of several interconnected units, and the system I am using to write this piece is not untypical with its main unit, separate keyboard, dot matrix printer, pen plotter, monitor, and mouse. All these peripherals connect to the main unit via the appropriate lead and port on the main unit. About half a dozen ports per computer would seem to be about "par for the course", but some of the better endowed machines (such as the BBC Model B) have a dozen or more.

In this chapter we will consider a number of the more common types of interface in some detail. This should help anyone who is trying to make up leads to interconnect two pieces of reasonably standard computer equipment, and should also help to avoid problems with trying to connect together two incompatible items of equipment. I referred to "reasonably standard" pieces of equipment above, rather than just "standard" equipment. Having used a large number of different computers and peripherals I have come to the conclusion that there is no such thing as a true computer standard. This may seem a bit cynical, but it is probably just being realistic about it rather than cynical! Many computer users have experienced problems in connecting together two pieces of gear that could reasonably be assumed to be totally compatible and easily used together. Things are actually much better now than they once were, as manufacturers have tended to fall in line with market leaders, and something close to true standards have emerged in some cases. There can still be unsuspected problems though. My advice is to use ready-made connecting cables as far as possible, even if you are experienced at electronics and making up cables. Ready-made cables can save a great deal of time and frustration, and in most cases are not too expensive these days.

Printer Ports

Printers are normally interfaced to computers via a parallel port, or a "Centronics" port as it is often called (presumably because it was originated by this company). Plotters are sometimes connected via a parallel port, but it is not used for many other types of equipment. In fact there are no other common items of equipment that use this type of interface, and apart from printers and plotters it is generally only used for special devices such as pieces of scientific equipment. Printers and plotters are often connected to computers by way of a serial interface. However, this is a general purpose type of port which is used with a wide range of equipment, and it is considered in a separate section of this chapter.

Data is sent to printers and most other computer peripherals in the form of eight bit binary numbers. With a parallel interface such as the Centronics type, each bit of data is carried by a separate wire. These are normally called "Data 0" to "Data 7", or more usually just "D0" to "D7" (or some similar abbreviation). In terms of the electrical signals carried by these wires, there are only two valid signal levels. The signal must be "high" (logic 1 or about 3 to 5 volts), or "low" (logic 0 or about 0 to 2 volts). In terms of ordinary decimal numbers, a line always represents 0 if it is at logic 0, or a certain value if it is set to logic 1. This list shows the values represented by each line when it is set to 1.

Line	Decimal Value
Data 0	1
Data 1	2
Data 2	4
Data 3	8
Data 4	16
Data 5	32
Data 6	64
Data 7	128

By setting up various bit patterns on the eight outputs it is possible to represent any decimal integer from 0 to 255. Exactly how each value is interpreted by the printer depends on the design of the printer. Most printers have a character set that is based on the ASCII (American Standard Codes for Information Interchange) set. For example, ASCII code number 85 is a "U" character. This is a subject that is covered in detail in another chapter, and it is not something that will be considered further here.

The eight data lines plus an earth connection enable values to be sent to the printer, but in practice more connecting lines are required. The first problem is that the printer must know when a new "byte" of data is ready to be read from the data lines. Otherwise it could read the same piece of data two or more times, or bytes of data could be missed altogether. The strobe line is used to indicate that new bytes of data are present on the data lines, and the signal on this line is a brief negative pulse (i.e. it is normally high, but it goes low for a short period when a new byte of data is present on the data lines).

There is a second problem in that a parallel interface is capable of transferring data at quite phenomenal rates. The maximum rate achievable depends on the exact hardware used, but a few hundred thousand bytes per second would be quite typical. Most printers can only print about 100 to 200 characters per second, and far less than this in the "near letter quality" mode. The printer therefore

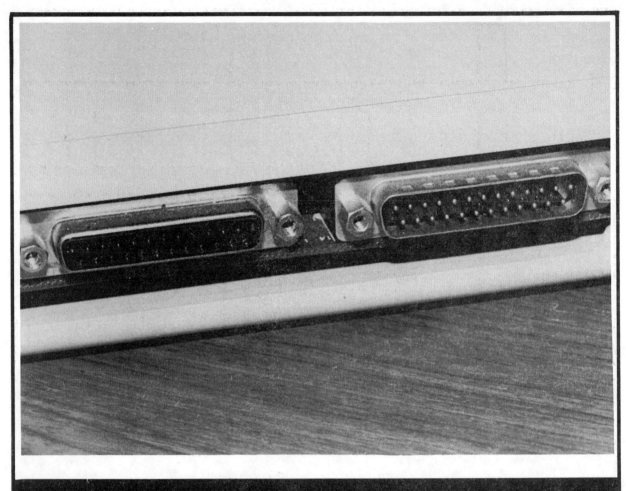

Standard IBM style parallel and serial ports. These are on an Amstrad PC1512, but other computers such as the Atari STs use the same connectors and basic method of connection.

needs some means of signalling to the computer whether or not it is ready to receive fresh data. It can then provide a hold-off during periods when it is processing received data, and is not ready to receive any more. This method of controlling the flow of data is known as "handshaking".

Parallel interfaces actually have two handshake lines, which are called "BUSY" and "ACKNOW-LEDGE". I am not quite sure why two handshake lines should be deemed necessary, since one would seem to be quite sufficient to control the flow of data correctly. In fact some computers have parallel printer interfaces that only implement one or the other of these lines (the BBC Model B series of computers only have the "acknowledge" handshake line for instance). They should both be present and fully operational on printers though. If we consider the acknowledge line first, this is normally in the high state. It stays at logic 1 when a byte of data has been received, but when this byte has been processed the "acknowledge" line is briefly taken low by the printer. The computer must therefore provide a fresh byte of data (if any data is ready to be sent)

each time it receives a negative pulse on the "acknowledge" line. The "busy" line is normally low, and it is set high by the printer when it receives a byte of data. It is set low again when the printer has processed the byte of data and is ready to receive the next one.

The timing diagram of Figure 2.1 shows typical waveforms for a parallel printer interface. You will note from this that the "acknowledge" and "busy" signals are very similar. In a few cases I have found it necessary to connect the "busy" input of the computer to the "acknowledge" output of the printer in order to obtain satisfactory results. However, this type of thing is a rarity, and normally the handshake outputs of the printer must be connected to the corresponding handshake inputs of the computer. In most cases connecting only one or the other of these lines will suffice, but if both inputs are implemented on the computer, then it is advisable to connect them both at the computer end of the system.

Figure 2.2 shows connection details for a standard parallel printer port. This shows the connector looking onto the port of a printer, or as it would be seen

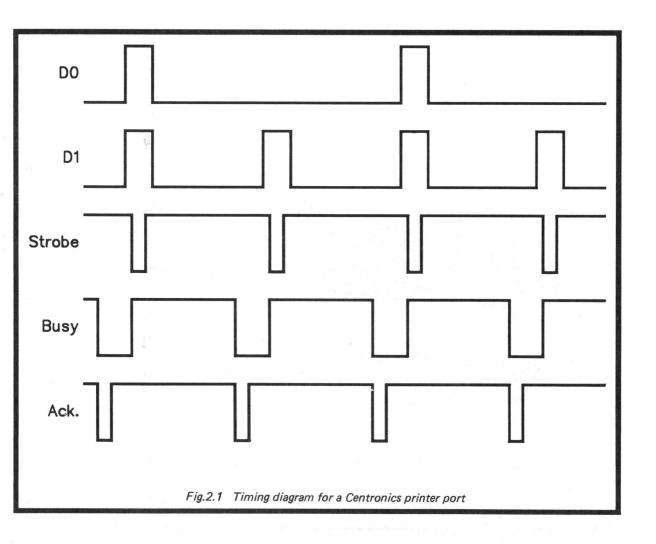

Fig.2.1 Timing diagram for a Centronics printer port

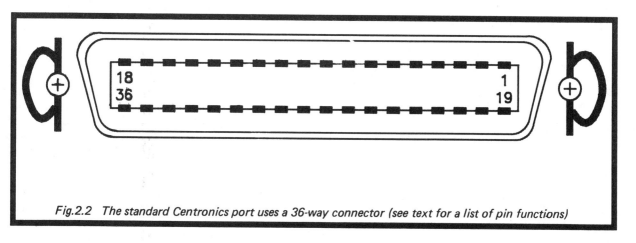

Fig.2.2 The standard Centronics port uses a 36-way connector (see text for a list of pin functions)

when connecting wires to the rear of a plug to fit a printer port. A 36 way connector is the standard one at the printer end of a parallel interface, and these are sometimes referred to as "Amphenol" 36 way connectors. More usually they are just called Centronics or parallel printer plugs and sockets (the printer has the plug – you need a socket to make the connections to it). This is a list of the parallel printer port connections.

Pin Number	Function	Input/Output
1	strobe	IN
2	Data 0	IN
3	Data 1	IN
4	Data 2	IN
5	Data 3	IN
6	Data 4	IN
7	Data 5	IN
8	Data 6	IN
9	Data 7	IN
10	Acknowledge	OUT
11	Busy	OUT
12	Paper Empty	OUT
13	+5V pull-up	OUT
14	Auto Line Feed	IN
15	No Connection	–
16	Ground	–
17	Chassis	–
18	No Connection	–
19 to 30	Ground	–
31	Init.	IN
32	Error	OUT
33	Ground	–
34	No Connection	–
35	+5V pull-up	OUT
36	SLCT	IN

Obviously there are a number of additional lines included here, and not just the basic data and handshake lines. A few terminals are not used, and a number of others are ground (or "earth") connections. There may seem to be no need for so many earth leads, and a single earth wire is in fact sufficient to wire the earths of the two pieces of equipment together. Several of the ground connections (notably 19 to 30) are needed to act as screens. Parallel printer cables are often made from "ribbon" cable, which has a number of leads side-by-side and a subsequent flat, ribbon-like appearance. When used with the appropriate (IDC) type of connectors, this results in a lead connected to ground separating one data lead from the next, and also separating the handshake lines. This helps to prevent stray coupling from one signal lead to another, and the corrupted data that this would produce.

Even with this simple system of screening, parallel printer interfaces are still only suitable for operation over relatively short distances. The maximum recom-

mended lead length is only some 2 metres. This is a bit restrictive, but is not unreasonable considering the very high rate at which data can be exchanged. It is not normally necessary to have printer leads much longer than this anyway, but in practice a lead 3 or 4 metres long would probably give perfectly acceptable results provided it is made using good quality materials.

Some of the other lines are not implemented on all computers/printers, or may have different functions. The ones shown here are those of my Epson printer, and are fairly typical these days. The "Paper Empty" line is an output from the printer that can be used to indicate to the computer that there is no paper in the printer, and that a hold-off is required. This is particularly useful when using a printer which is hand-fed with single sheets, but by no means all computers and software support this feature (it does seem to be implemented by IBM PCs/XTs/ATs and compatibles, plus most of the software that runs on them). It is a feature that is not supported by most home computers.

The "Auto Line Feed" input of a printer is normally taken high, but is taken low if each carriage return must be accompanied by a line feed. A common problem when first using a printer is that of either everything being printed on the same line, or of double line spacing being obtained when only single line spacing has been set. Everything being printed on one line occurs when neither the printer nor the computer add a line feed after each carriage return. The double spacing occurs when they both add the line feed. The "Auto Line Feed" input is not often used, or needed. It is usually possible to set the software to suit the default line feed setting of the printer. Failing that, there are usually DIP switches somewhere on (or in) the printer that can be used to over-ride this input and set the appropriate operating condition.

In some cases the "Error" output is used to indicate that the printer has detected what could genuinely be termed an error, but in most cases it simply goes low when the printer is out of paper, or it is merely switched "off-line". The "Init" input is pulsed low in order to initialise the printer. In other words, a low pulse on this input takes the printer to its normal switch-on state. This effectively counteracts any control signals it has been sent, such as switching it to a graphics mode, switching on bold type, or something of this nature.

The SLCT input enables printer select and deselect codes when it is taken high, and disables them when it is taken low. This is another input that can usually be over-ridden by a DIP switch on the printer. The +5 volt pull-up terminals are used if there is an unused input on either the printer or the computer that must be taken high rather than low (any unused lines which must be taken low are simply connected to a ground terminal). These two terminals are not normally required.

Computer End

In theory, each terminal of the printer's parallel port is connected to the corresponding terminal of the computer's parallel port. In practice things are not always so straightforward. One potential problem is the lack of either an "acknowledge" or "busy" terminal at the computer end of the system. This does not really matter, and it is just a matter of connecting which one happens to be present. Either one of these handshake lines should be sufficient to give a properly regulated flow of data from the computer to the printer.

What is a more difficult problem is that there is no properly standardised connector for the computer end of a parallel printer interface. There may be a computer that uses a standard 36 way Amphenol connector here, but I have never come across one. The nearest thing to a standard connector at the computer end of a parallel printer link is the 25 way D type connector as used on the IBM PC/XT/AT and compatibles. This is also used on the Atari ST range of computers, and the later versions of the Commodore Amiga. Note that the original Amiga (the "1000") has a 25 way D connector for its parallel printer port, but that this is a plug rather than the socket of the IBMs etc. Details of the standard IBM style printer port are shown in Figure 2.3, with the

Amiga 1000 version shown in Figure 2.4. In common with most computer printer ports, the basic layout of the connections roughly matches that of the 36 way connector at the printer. This makes things very much easier for the do-it-yourself printer lead constructor. I doubt if the do-it-yourself approach is worthwhile with an IBM printer lead. Buying the two connectors and a piece of multi-way lead could easily cost more than a ready-made lead! As these leads are so popular, the ready-made ones mostly sell for just a few pounds each.

The BBC model B computers (including the B Plus, Master 128, etc.) have a 26 way IDC connector at the parallel printer port. The computer has a plug, and the lead must therefore be terminated in a 26 way IDC header socket. Details of this port are shown in Figure 2.5. Note that in its unexpanded form the BBC model A computer does not have a printer port. Several home computers have used IDC connectors for their printer ports, including the Oric and Oric Atmos (Fig.2.6) and one or two other obsolete models.

The Amstrad CPC series of computers have a built-in printer port which uses an edge connector (which is just a simple connector formed by part of the machine's printed circuit board). Details of this port are provided in Figure 2.7. Connections to this are

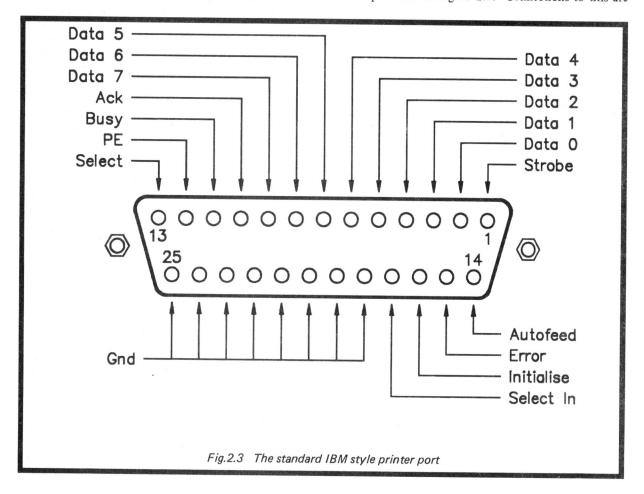

Fig.2.3 The standard IBM style printer port

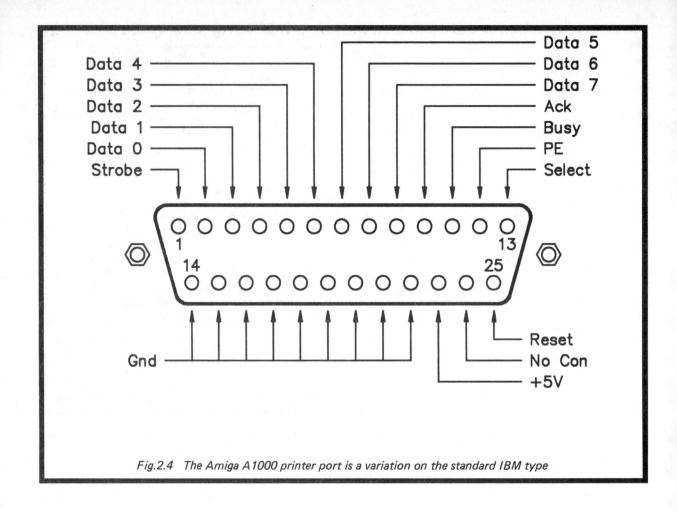

Fig.2.4   The Amiga A1000 printer port is a variation on the standard IBM type

by way of a 2 x 17 way 0.1 inch pitch edge connector which should ideally be fitted with a polarising key at the correct position so that the connector can not be fitted the wrong way round. Like most home computer printer ports, it is fairly basic and has an absolute minimum of connections. A point worth noting about the Amstrad CPC printer port is that data line 7 is simply connected to earth at the computer. This means that the computer can not send values of more than 127 to the printer. The ASCII set does not use values above this figure, and most printer control codes do not require any values above 127. However, some printers do have features that can only be accessed using values of 128 to 255, and these are not available from any computer which only provides a seven bit output.

The MSX computers have an unusual connector for their printer ports. This is a 14 way Amphenol connector, which is a sort of miniature and cut down version of the standard 36 way parallel printer connector. Details of the MSX printer port are shown in Figure 2.8. A home-made MSX printer lead should be easy enough to make up, but a suitable 14 way connector for the computer end of the lead could be difficult to obtain.

Connections
The main point to watch when making up a printer lead is that at the very least the "strobe", eight data lines, one ground terminal, and either "acknowledge" or "busy" are interconnected. As explained previously, it is a good idea to have ground leads to screen the data and handshake lines from one another, especially if the lead is going to be more than about half a metre in length. Three or four metres is the maximum length of cable you are likely to get away with in practice, and the maximum recommended cable length is only two metres. Do not try a cable of more than two metres in length unless you really need a longer cable.

A printer will normally work properly if an unused input (such as "Init" or "Auto Line Feed") is left unconnected. Problems should only arise if one of these inputs is taken to a ground terminal on the computer's port when it should be allowed to "float" to the high state. For example, pin 14 of the Amstrad CPC printer port is connected to ground, but this terminal of many Epson printers is the "Auto Line Feed" input. To avoid unwanted double line spacing these two terminals should not be linked, and with a ready-made cable that links these two terminals

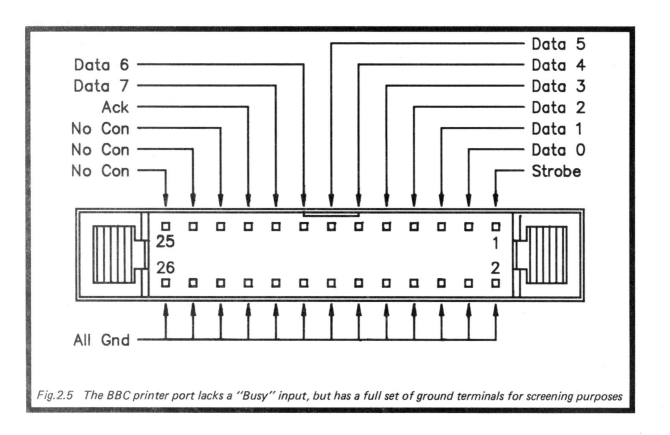

Fig.2.5   The BBC printer port lacks a "Busy" input, but has a full set of ground terminals for screening purposes

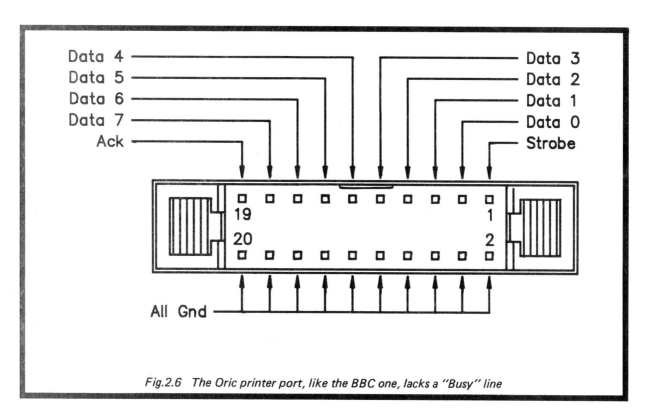

Fig.2.6   The Oric printer port, like the BBC one, lacks a "Busy" line

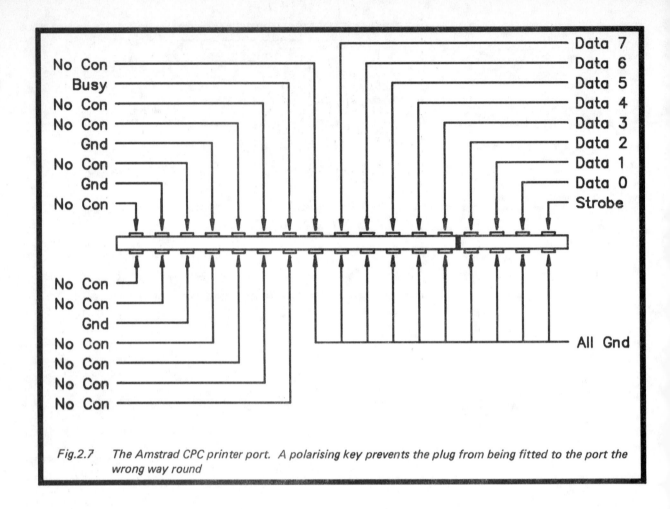

Fig.2.7   The Amstrad CPC printer port. A polarising key prevents the plug from being fitted to the port the wrong way round

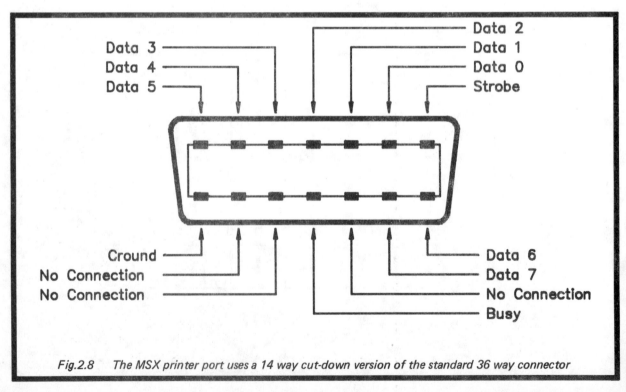

Fig.2.8   The MSX printer port uses a 14 way cut-down version of the standard 36 way connector

it could be beneficial to carefully cut the wire that connects them. If the handshaking does not provide a proper hold-off, make sure that either the "acknowledge" or "busy" terminals are properly linked. If linking one set of terminals does not have the desired effect, try linking the other set as well. If that fails, try connecting "busy" on one unit to "acknowledge" on the other. It sometimes provides a cure, and it should certainly not harm either piece of equipment.

Another point to watch is that the lead is not short circuiting a power supply output to earth. If this should happen it is likely that the overload protection in the equipment providing the supply output would prevent any damage from occurring, but it is best not to find out! There is not usually any problem with +5 volt pull-up outputs, as they normally have a current limiting resistor that enables them to be connected to earth with only a very small output current flowing. Greater care needs to be taken with a computer such as the Commodore Amiga 1000, where pin 23 of its printer port is a proper 5 volt supply output. Obviously an output of this type must be left unconnected, or it should be connected to a "No Connection" ("NC") terminal on the other piece of equipment.

A possible cause of confusion is that some manufacturer's connection diagrams identify the data lines as "Data 1" to "Data 8", not "Data 0" to "Data 7". In this case "Data 0" connects to "Data 1", "Data 1" connects to "Data 2", and so on, through to "Data 7" which connects to "Data 8".

Serial Ports

A parallel printer port is fine for its intended applications, but it has a couple of major shortcomings as a general purpose computer interface. The most obvious one is that it provides only one-way communications. I suppose that this is not insurmountable, and could be overcome by having devices equipped with both a parallel input and a parallel output. The second problem is a more serious one, and is the limited operating range. If you want to connect a computer to a piece of equipment in another room, the chances are that a parallel interface will not be able to give reliable results over the modest range involved. A related problem is that a large number of connecting leads are required, and this makes long parallel connecting cables prohibitively expensive.

The standard general purpose computer communications interface is the RS232C serial type. In its most basic form this requires just two connecting leads. These are the signal lead plus a ground connection. Clearly it is not possible to send eight bits of data at once with only one data line available. Instead, the data must be sent one bit at a time. The least significant bit is sent first (i.e. the "Data 0" signal), running through in sequence to the most significant bit (the "Data 7" signal). The receiving device must monitor the state of the data line at regular intervals so that it can determine the state of each bit and reconstitute the eight bit byte of data.

For this system to work it is essential that the receiving device samples the data line at intervals that match those at which the transmitting equipment places fresh data onto the data line. This is achieved by having data sent at standard rates, or "baud" rates as they are termed. There are a number of standard baud rates, and it is obviously important that the transmitting and receiving devices are set for the same rate. The normal baud rates are 45.45, 50, 75, 110, 150, 300, 600, 1200, 1800, 2400, 3600, 4800, 9600, and 19200 baud. The baud rate is merely the number of bits sent per second with continuous transmission.

Having standard baud rates only partially solves the problem of synchronisation. The receiving device must know when to start reading in bits for a new byte of data. One way of tackling the problem is to have an extra connecting wire which carries some form of synchronisation signal. This is normally in the form of pulses which indicate when each bit of data should be read from the data line. This is known as a "synchronous" serial link, and there are some interfaces of this type in use. They are relatively rare though, and most serial links, including the RS232C type, are of the "asynchronous" variety. These have the synchronisation signals placed on the same line as the data.

In fact the RS232C system uses only one synchronisation signal which is transmitted at the beginning of each byte. As one would reasonably expect, this is called the "start" bit. This change from the data line's normal quiescent state to the active one indicates to the receiving equipment that it must sample the data line at regular intervals thereafter until a full byte of data has been read in and converted back to parallel data.

There are also "stop" bits, but these are not really for synchronisation purposes. During the stop bits the signal line is at its normal quiescent level, and these just provide a minimum gap between bytes. Apart from giving the receiving device time to do something with each decoded byte before starting to read in the next one, this ensures that the data line is in the quiescent state prior to each start bit, so that the receiving equipment can recognise each start bit.

One further complication is parity checking. This seems to be little used in practice, although many serial devices are equipped to use it. The general idea is that there should always be an even number of bits set to one in each byte (even parity), or there should always be an odd number of bits set to one (odd parity). Obviously the character codes will not conform to either standard without some help from the serial interface, which must add a bit to some codes in order to produce an odd or even number of bits, as required. The point of doing this is that a very simple error checking circuit at the receiving end of the system can be used to detect an odd number of

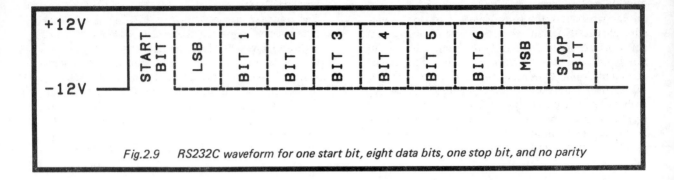

Fig.2.9   RS232C waveform for one start bit, eight data bits, one stop bit, and no parity

bits when there should be an even number, or vice versa. This method of error checking is not very sophisticated though, and a double glitch can result in the wrong character being produced, but with the correct parity being detected. Any parity bits added by the serial interface are placed after the last data bit and before the stop bit or bits.

The waveform diagram of Figure 2.9 helps to show the way in which serial data is encoded onto a single data line. Note that the signal voltages used for RS232C signals are not the standard 5 volt logic levels. They are nominally plus and minus 12 volts, but under full load (i.e. when connected to a serial input via a long cable) signal voltages as low as plus and minus 3 volts are acceptable.

RS232C signals should never be connected direct to inputs that are only intended for operation with normal logic levels. The user ports of the Commodore 64 and VIC-20 computers can be used as RS232C interfaces, but they are only designed to send and receive standard logic levels. Also, they provide signals of the wrong polarity. They require an interface unit which provides signal inversions and voltage shifting for operation with standard RS232C equipment. A few items of equipment have inputs and outputs that are suitable for operation with logic level serial signals such as those provided by the Commodore 64 and VIC-20 user ports.

Word Formats

There are a lot of possible word formats with serial interfaces, and more than you might expect from the above description. One universal factor is that there is always one start bit. There can be anything from five to eight data bits though, and one or two stop bits. If five data bits are used, there is normally one or one and a half stop bits (not two). Then there can be odd parity, even parity, or (more usually) no parity used at all. In a computing context word formats having less than seven bits are not normally used as they would not be able to handle the seven bit ASCII codes. A few seven bit word formats were at one time quite common, but they seem to have largely given way to eight bit formats in recent times.

Much computer communications requires the interchange of eight bit codes, and this is obviously not possible with a seven bit word format.

Before two pieces of equipment can be successfully linked via their RS232C interfaces it is clearly necessary to get both interfaces set for the same word format and an identical baud rate. It does not matter too much which word format is used, except where eight bit codes must be exchanged. Obviously an eight bit word format is then required. In the interest of a speedy data exchange, a word format which has just one stop bit and no parity is best. This would all seem to indicate that a word format of one start bit, eight data bits, one stop bit, and no parity is the best one for general purpose computer use. This does seem to be emerging as the most popular word format. Remember that the baud rate is the number bits sent per second, not the number of bytes. With one start bit, eight data bits, and one stop bit, there is a total of ten bits per byte. A baud rate of (say) 1200 baud therefore provides an absolute maximum data transfer rate of 120 bytes per second.

For speedy data transfer a high baud rate is obviously best, but there are a couple of points to keep in mind here. The first one is that a high baud rate is rather pointless if either the transmitting or receiving equipment can not handle large amounts of data in a short space of time. The same thing is true if data will only be sent in short and very intermittent bursts. The rate of data exchange would then be limited by other parts of the system and not the serial interfaces. Most of the time the interfaces would be idle. It would then be better to use a lower baud rate, as this would not make the overall system significantly slower, and it should give better reliability.

The second point to bear in mind is that the higher the baud rate, the lower the maximum range of the system. RS232C systems are guaranteed to operate over a range of at least 15 metres at 19200 baud. Probably this is sufficient for the vast majority of applications, but lower baud rates permit much longer ranges to be achieved. For very long ranges the serial signals are usually tone encoded/decoded using a modem (a subject covered in detail elsewhere in this book).

Multi-Wire Systems

So far we have only considered a basic one signal wire plus earth system, for one-way communication. An RS232C interface has both input and output terminals, and is therefore capable of two-way communication. It is just a matter of interconnecting the earths of the two interfaces, and cross-coupling their input and output terminals. A basic two way system of this type is suitable for some applications, including most modem communications systems. However, some applications require handshake lines.

Practical Ports

The standard connector for an RS232C is a 25 way D connector which has the method of pin numbering shown in Figure 2.11. Note that this diagram shows the pin numbering when looking onto a computer's RS232C port (which normally has a male connector), or looking onto the rear of a socket to fit an RS232C port. This type of connector is used on many computers and other items of equipment, including the IBM PC/XT and compatibles, and the Atari ST range. However, not all the terminals are necessarily

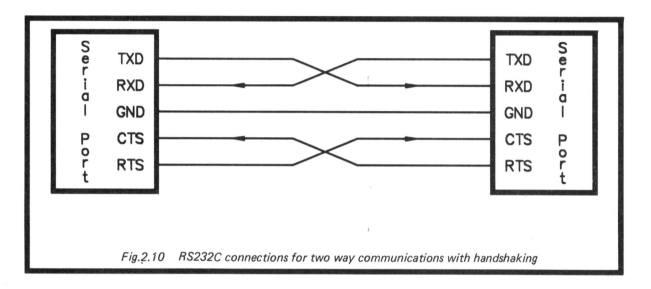

Fig.2.10   RS232C connections for two way communications with handshaking

A two-way RS232C setup with handshaking in both directions would use the method of connection shown in Figure 2.10. This is the basic earth plus two signal wires, with the other two leads providing the handshaking (two leads as there is separate handshaking in each direction). RS232C interfaces have a reputation for being difficult to get properly connected and fully operational. In part the problem is due to the variety of word formats and baud rates in use, and getting one end of the system to properly match the other.

The main cause of problems seems to be the connecting cable, and getting the handshake lines properly sorted out. In the simple example system of Figure 2.10 the flow of data from terminal 2 to terminal 1 is controlled by the "RTS" ("Request To Send") output. This goes positive when terminal 1 is ready to receive data, and negative when it is not. This output is read by the "CTS" ("Clear To Send") input on terminal 2, and hardware oɪ a mixture of hardware and software at terminal 2 provides a hold-off when necessary. The handshaking in the opposite direction uses the same arrangement. There are alternative handshake lines on an RS232C interface, and "DTR" ("Data Terminal Ready") can be used instead of "RTS", and "DSR" ("Data Set Ready") may be used instead of "CTS".

implemented. In particular the various "secondary" connections are often omitted, and are not really needed. They are only included as back-ups to the primary connections. The terminals that carry timing signals only need to be implemented in synchronous serial systems, but all computer RS232C interfaces seem to be of the asynchronous type.

This list is for the full RS232C implementation.

Pin No.	Function	Input/Output
1	Protective Ground	—
2	Transmitted Data	OUT
3	Received Data	IN
4	Request To Send (RTS)	OUT
5	Clear To Send (CTS)	IN
6	Data Set Ready (DSR)	IN
7	Signal Ground	—
8	Data Carrier Detect (DCD)	IN
9	Reserved For Data Set Testing	—
10	Reserved For Data Set Testing	—
11	Not Used	—
12	Sec. Rec. Line Sig. Det.	—
13	Secondary CTS	—
14	Secondary Transmitted Data	—

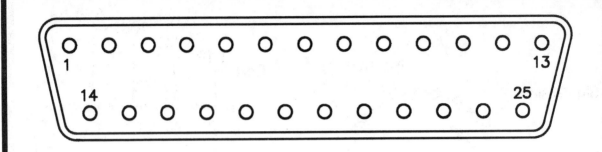

Fig.2.11   Pin numbering for the standard RS232C connector

Pin No.	Function	Intput/Output
15	Transmission Signal Element Timing	–
16	Secondary Received Data	–
17	Receiver Signal Element Timing	–
18	Not Used	–
19	Secondary Request To Send	–
20	Data Terminal Ready (DTR)	OUT
21	Signal Quality Detector	–
22	Ring Indicator	IN
23	Data Signal Rate Selector	–
24	Transmit Signal Element Timing	–
25	Not Used	–

A lot of serial ports are substantially cut down versions of the full system. The RS232C interface was designed as a general purpose type not intended specifically for computer use, and it has a number of functions that are of little or no value in computing applications. As explained previously, as little as five terminals (ground, data input, data output, and two handshake lines) are sufficient for a basic two way link with handshaking. Computer RS232C ports often use a different type of connector. This is understandable, since the 25 terminals of the standard D connector are unnecessary with perhaps only five or six terminals actually being implemented. On the other hand, it does mean that standard RS232C connecting leads are unusable with these ports (although ready-made serial leads for many non-standard ports are available).

Figure 2.12 provides connection details for the serial ports of IBM AT and compatible computers, and the Epson LQ800 printer. These use a 9 way D connector and a 6 way DIN type respectively. The LQ800 only needs to receive data, and it has what is basically just a data input, handshake output, and

earth connections. This should be quite sufficient though. Note that an adaptor is available for AT computers, and this couples the 9 way D connector to a standard 25 way type (an adaptor of this type was supplied with my AT compatible, but it is apparently not always included as standard).

If a ready-made serial lead for your equipment can not be obtained, or you are determined to make up your own lead, the first thing is to ensure that the ground terminals of the two ports are inter-connected, and that the data input/output terminals are cross connected. If only a one-way link is required, such as when driving a printer from a computer, then obviously only one data input to data output connection is required. It is advisable to check equipment manuals to determine whether or not equipment is genuinely of the one-way type. A lot of plotters have serial ports, and some of these (notably the Hewlett-Packard and truely compatible types) can operate in modes where they output data to the computer! The data link from the plotter back to the printer may still not be needed though, since most software seems to ignore this facility. I have encountered one or two pieces of software that will only drive a plotter if full two-way communications is provided.

In some cases handshaking will not be needed, and no further connections will be required. Handshaking is often unnecessary when using a computer with a modem, and at modest baud rates it may not be needed when transferring data from one computer to another. It is almost certain to be needed with printers, plotters, or any relatively slow device. The only exceptions are when the device receiving data has a large buffer. It may then be able to read in data at a very high rate, and a hold-off will only become necessary if the buffer should become filled. If handshaking is not required, the handshake lines can usually be ignored. This is not always the case though, and sometimes a serial port will not output data unless one of the handshake inputs (or the data carrier detect terminal) is tied to a particular signal

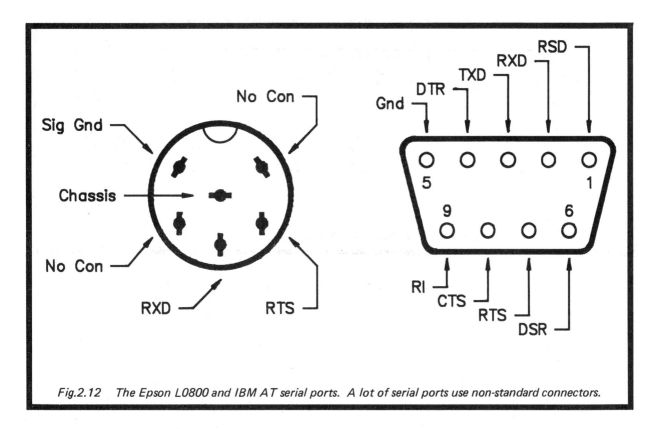

Fig.2.12   The Epson LO800 and IBM AT serial ports. A lot of serial ports use non-standard connectors.

level. You may then need to implement one hand-shake interconnection, even though it will always enable the data flow and will never go into the hold-off state. If equipment refuses to provide a flow of data for no apparent reason it is certainly worth trying it with the handshake lines connected. Some serial interfaces have a +12 volt output which is intended as a tie-point for a handshake line that must be permanently enabled. Any terminal of this kind is not a standard RS232C signal, and would usually utilize one of the normally unused terminals rather than replacing one of the assigned but not required functions.

Where handshaking must be implemented there are a number of possible methods of connection, and sometimes it is necessary to adopt a "suck it and see" approach in order to get satisfactory results. There are devices called RS232C "break-out" boxes which enable changes in the method of interconnection to be made quickly and easily, plus an array of diagnostic devices for use when struggling with RS232C links. Be careful not to get two outputs connected together. The RS232C standard stipulates that current limiting should be used at outputs, and getting two outputs connected together should not cause any damage. Nevertheless, with any interfacing it is still best to avoid this type of mistake if possible. The connection diagram of Figure 2.13 shows two methods of interconnection. Both are quite simple and will be successful in most cases (I have used the method of connection shown in (a)

on several occasions without encountering any difficulty).

One final but important point to note is that there are two types of RS232C port. These are the "data communications equipment" ("DCE") and "data terminal equipment" ("DTE") types. Most RS232C ports encountered in computing are of the DTE variety, which is the normal type where the port transmits on its "data out" terminal, and receives on its "data in" terminal. DCE equipment has a port which is the opposite of this, with data being transmitted on the input terminal, and received on the output terminal.

The idea is that by having pieces of equipment of opposite types, they can be connected by a cable which has each pin of one socket connected to the same pin on the other socket (i.e. not the usual cross coupling of most pins). You are unlikely to encounter DCE equipment, but it might be worthwhile checking manuals to ensure that "data out" is the function of that pin, and not the terminal it must connect to on the other port. The only DCE RS232C port I can remember encountering was on a Sinclair QL computer that had two serial ports, with one configured as a DTE port and the other connected as a DCE type. This permitted easy connection to any piece of equipment having an RS232C port (in theory anyway). It is important to realise that there is no fundamental difference between DTE and DCE equipment. They only differ in the way in which they are wired up to the 25 way D connec-

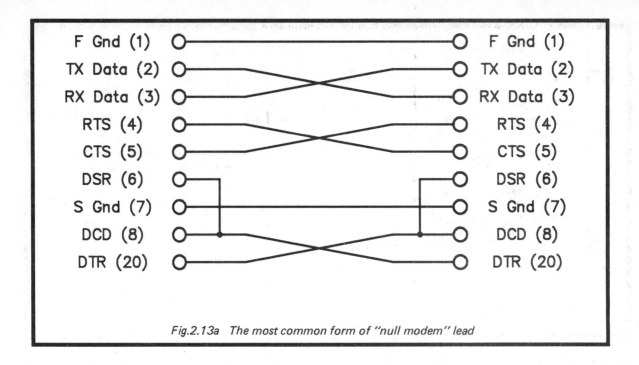

Fig.2.13a   The most common form of "null modem" lead

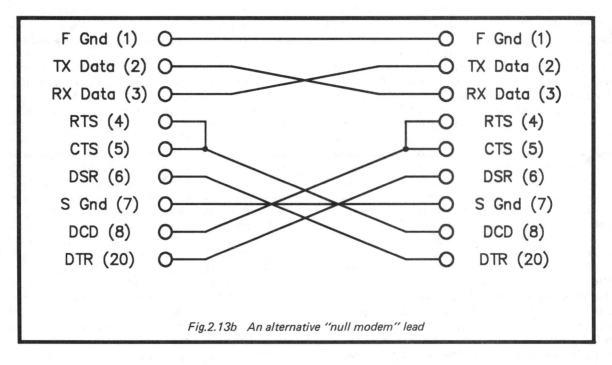

Fig.2.13b   An alternative "null modem" lead

tor. An adaptor cable is all that is needed in order to convert one type to the other. The two cables of Figure 2.13 will in fact convert one type of port to the other. This type of cross-coupled RS232C cable is usually termed a "null modem" cable incidentally.

Other Serial Systems

There are other forms of serial link which have been devised in an attempt to improve on the performance of the RS232C type. This generally means longer range, for a given baud rate, and higher maximum baud rates. Probably the best known of these alternative serial interfaces is the RS423 type (not the RS432 type as it is often referred to). This is used on the BBC model B and Master series of computers, and was also used on the Enterprise computers. Connection details for the BBC and Enterprise serial ports are shown in Figure 2.14.

The RS423 interface is essentially a streamlined version of the RS232C type, with the little-used

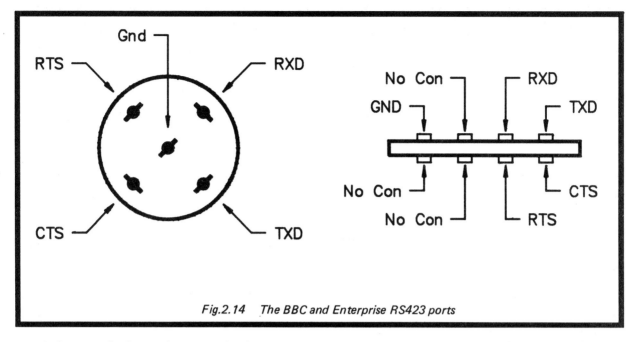

Fig.2.14   The BBC and Enterprise RS423 ports

terminals omitted. It uses lower signal voltages and a higher drive current, and it is more tolerant of any distortion of the signal. This helps to give greater range for a given baud rate. The minimum signal voltage is still sufficient to drive RS232C inputs, and an RS423 input can take the higher voltages of an RS232C type. The two types are therefore compatible provided the baud rates and word formats can be matched properly.

There is a more advanced serial interface in the form of the RS422 type. This is capable of very high speed operation due to the use of a balanced line technique (i.e. the signal is carried by two lines which carry signals that are the opposite of one another). There is another high speed serial system in the form of the RS449 type. Other "improved" RS232C interfaces have been suggested from time to time, but the standard RS232C type is still far more common than any of the alternatives.

MIDI

MIDI is an acronym of "Musical Instrument Digital Interface", and it is a means of connecting two electronic musical instruments together. This is normally done so that playing on one instrument also plays the second (or any number of additional instruments). It can be used for other purposes though, such as exchanging sound data between instruments, or recording tracks of music into a sequencer and playing them back into a MIDI instrument or instruments. This is rather like a cross between multi-track tape recording and a player piano, but is potentially much more versatile than either of these.

At first sight MIDI might not seem to have much to do with computing, but a few computers have a built-in MIDI interface (the Atari ST series for example), and it is an add-on that is available for many more computers. With suitable software a computer can make an excellent sequencer, and computer based sequencers are probably superior to dedicated units in most respects. Computers can also be used to good effect in other MIDI applications, such as MIDI data processing. MIDI is therefore very much an important part of modern computing.

From the technical point of view MIDI is very similar to an RS232C interface, but it is not compatible with an RS232C interface. In some cases it is possible to add a simple adaptor to an RS232C interface so that with suitable software it can operate as a MIDI port. This is the system normally used with the Commodore Amiga computer for instance. In most cases this approach is not possible because MIDI uses a non-standard baud rate of 31250 baud. The hardware in some computers can actually be set for this baud rate, and these could be used with a simple adaptor. This would probably only be worthwhile if matching software is also available. The MIDI word format is the common one of one start bit, eight data bits, one stop bit, and no parity.

An important difference between MIDI and the RS232C standard is that MIDI uses a current loop signal and not two different voltages to represent the two logic levels. MIDI uses a current flow of zero to represent one logic level, and a current flow of 5 milliamps (a small fraction of that consumed by the average torch bulb) to represent the other. Connecting a MIDI interface to a RS232C type is not likely to damage either piece of equipment, but it is not likely to give the desired result. MIDI inputs use opto-isolators to couple the signal into the equipment without having any direct electrical connection between the driving device and the main circuit of the driven equipment. This avoids potential problems with mains "hum" or other noise being produced on

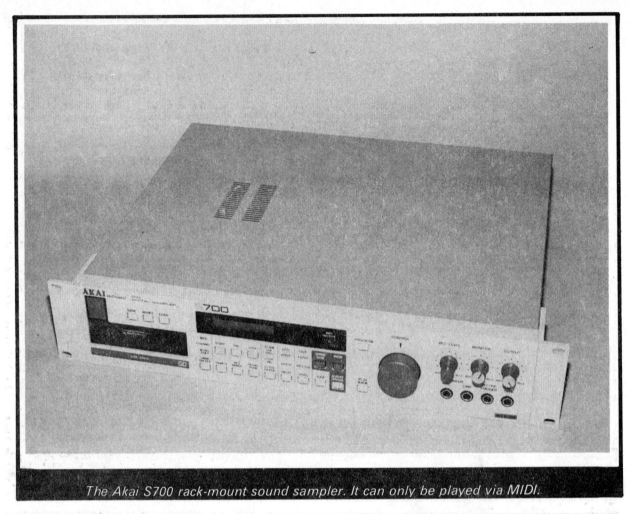

The Akai S700 rack-mount sound sampler. It can only be played via MIDI.

the audio outputs of equipment in the system, and it also eliminates any risk of damage occurring due to the earths of two pieces of equipment being at different voltages.

MIDI interfacing is much more straightforward than RS232C interfacing. A factor that helps to greatly simplify matters is that MIDI does not use any form of handshaking. This is not quite true, as MIDI does under certain circumstances use software handshaking, where the start/stop messages are passed via the data in/data out connections and not by way of separate lines (a system sometimes used with RS232C interfaces incidentally). MIDI does not use hardware handshaking with handshake connections though. This gives just three wires to connect one MIDI device to another. Two of these are the signal wires, and the third is the earth connection. Note that the earth connection is only connected internally at MIDI outputs, and is left unconnected at inputs. This is due to the isolation used at inputs, which would be bypassed by the earth connection if it was connected at both ends of the system. The only reason for using the earth lead is to provide screening of the signal wires so that they do not radiate significant amounts of radio

frequency interference. MIDI leads are made from twin screened lead, with the inner conductors carrying the signals, and the outer braiding connected to earth so that it provides the screening. The problem of radiating radio frequency interference is not one that is peculiar to MIDI connecting cables. RS232C and parallel printer cables are also potential sources of interference, and should really be properly screened in order to minimise the problem.

Apart from MIDI "IN" and "OUT" sockets there is also the "THRU" variety. This is a form of MIDI output, and it simply sends out any signal received on the MIDI input. The idea of this is to permit several pieces of equipment to be connected together in "chain" fashion, so that one controller can be used in conjunction with several instruments. Figure 2.15 shows a typical setup of this type.

The standard connector for MIDI interfaces is the 5 way 180 degree DIN type. The MIDI standard also sanctions the use of the higher quality XLR type connectors, but only if manufacturers make available optional adaptors to permit standard MIDI (DIN type) leads to be used with their equipment that uses XLR connectors. In practice there seems to be very little equipment that does not use the standard DIN

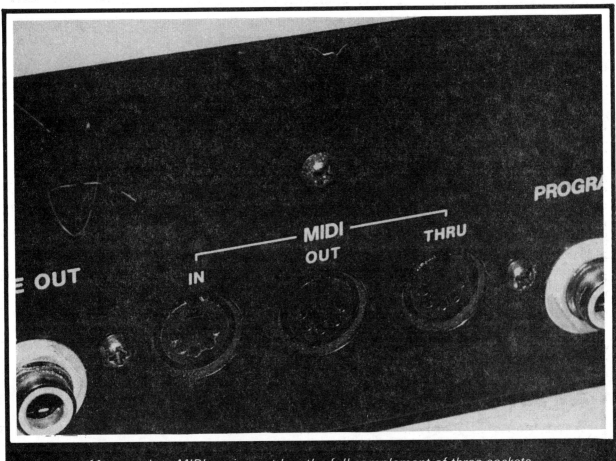

*Most modern MIDI equipment has the full complement of three sockets.
The THRU socket is absent on some keyboard instruments though (especially older types).*

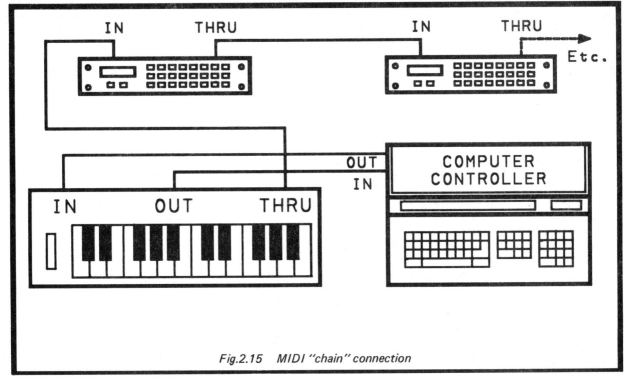

Fig.2.15   MIDI "chain" connection

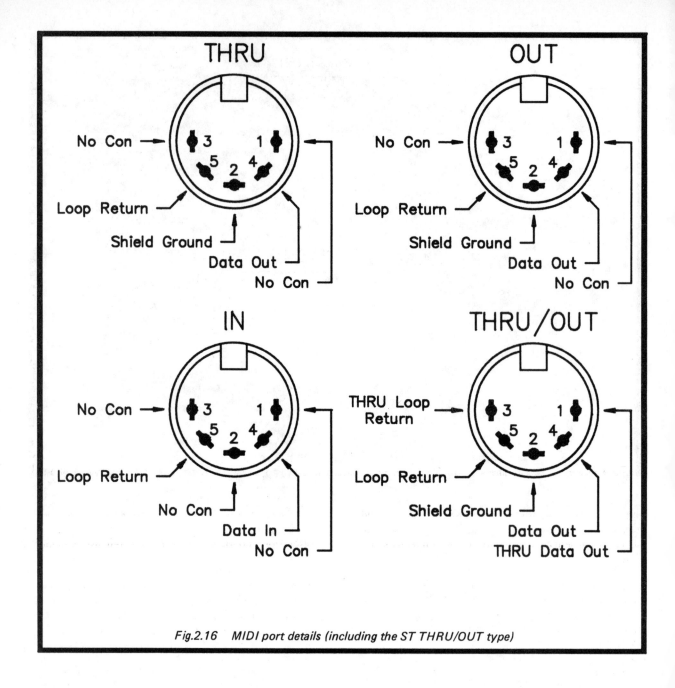

Fig.2.16   MIDI port details (including the ST THRU/OUT type)

connectors. Connection details for all three types of MIDI port are provided in Figure 2.16. This also gives details of the non-standard arrangement used on the OUT/THRU socket of the Atari ST computers. This can in fact be used as a standard MIDI OUT provided the THRU facility is not required. The THRU facility is provided by the two normally unused terminals of the OUT socket. A non-standard lead is needed if the THRU facility of the ST is to be used (often it will not be required), but larger ST dealers can probably supply a suitable lead. Do-it-yourself MIDI leads are not difficult to make up, and Figure 2.17 shows the wiring needed.

Monitors
Like so many aspects of computing, there are standards for monitors, but a number of them, and not all monitors conform to one of these standards. The most simple type of monitor interface is the composite video type which conforms to the broadcast standard. In other words, a monitor of this type will work just as well with the composite video output of a video recorder (or other item of video equipment) as it will with a computer that has the appropriate type of output. This interface has just two terminals which carry the earth and single signal connections. The horizontal sychronisation, vertical

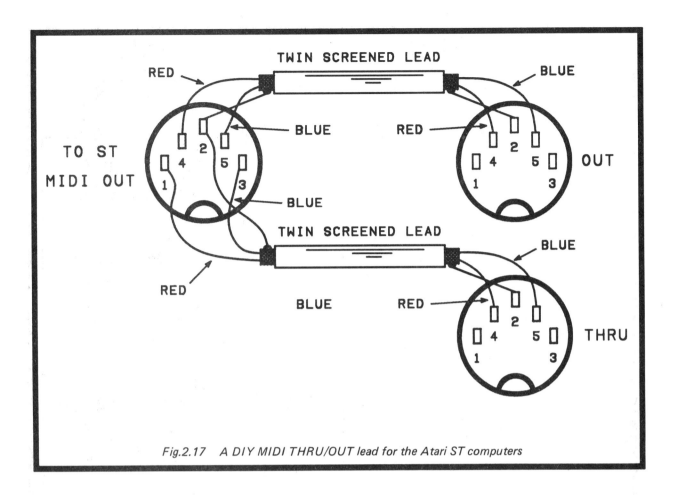

RED

TWIN SCREENED LEAD

BLUE

TO ST
MIDI OUT

BLUE

RED

OUT

BLUE

BLUE

TWIN SCREENED LEAD

BLUE

RED

BLUE

RED

THRU

Fig.2.17   A DIY MIDI THRU/OUT lead for the Atari ST computers

synchronisation, and main picture signal are all mixed in together with this type of interface, but any audio signal is carried by a separate set of connectors and lead.

Sound is something that should be borne in mind when selecting a monitor for a computer that does not have a built-in loudspeaker for its sound generator. With a computer of this type there will be no audio output unless the monitor has an audio input (which might not actually matter too much, particularly if the computer is only needed for something like word processing).

Composite video outputs seem to be used mainly with monochrome monitors, and there seems to be a popular myth that they are only suitable for this type of signal. In actual fact a composite signal can include colour information, and with computers such as the Commodore Amiga and Atari ST a colour signal is provided by their composite outputs. In fact colour can be handled very well by a composite video output, with an infinite colour range available. As we shall see shortly, some other types of monitor interface permit only a very restricted range of colours to be displayed. Do not assume that a composite video output is always a colour type, as not all computers necessarily put any colour information on this output signal.

Not all systems that use composite signals conform to the broadcast signal standard. In particular, high resolution monochrome systems often use a higher frame rate than the broadcast standard of 50 frames per second. Although there are fifty frames per second, each frame consists of only every other line of the display. Consequently, two frames are needed to make each complete picture, and there are only twenty-five frames per second. With high resolution screens this system tends to give a very pronounced flickering, especially if it is used to display high contrast pictures or pictures having large bright areas. Interlacing helps to minimise the flickering, but it does not eliminate it. This effect can be seen when using the Commodore Amiga computer with one of its modes that have a vertical resolution of 400 lines (or 512 lines on the PAL versions). A long persistence monitor is one solution to the problem, but a higher scan rate (often without interlacing) is a better one. As an example, the high resolution monochrome mode of the Atari ST computers has a vertical scan frequency of 72 Hertz, and gives a very stable picture. Although broadcast standard composite input monitors can be used in the two colour modes of the Atari ST computers, a special monitor is required for the high resolution monochrome mode (which uses a separate output terminal of the video

35

port). It is not safe to assume that the composite input of a monitor is suitable for use with high resolution displays.

RGB

Most colour monitors do not have a composite input, or do have one, but are normally driven from another input wherever possible. The alternative input is almost invariably some form of RGB (red-green-blue) input. It should perhaps be pointed out that some monochrome monitors have an RGB input, but obviously they can not provide a colour display. They will usually display the colours as different shades of grey though, which is a definite improvement on a true monochrome display. However, in some cases there is very little difference between many of the shades of grey, and the IBM colour graphics adaptor (and compatible display adaptors) often provide disappointing results when used with monochrome monitors. This is not really a fault in the video board, which is obviously optimised for true colour operation.

With an RGB input there are several input signals to the monitor. For a basic RGB monitor with TTL inputs (i.e. standard logic signal inputs) there are normally five inputs plus an earth terminal. The five inputs are red, green, blue, intensity, and composite synchronisation (i.e. horizontal and vertical synchronisation signals merged into a single signal). Anyone who studied physics at school will probably realise the importance of having red, green, and blue signals. The classic colour experiment is to project three circles of light onto a white screen, with the circles overlapping slightly. Coloured filters are used to produce red, green, and blue circles of light. This gives the result shown in Figure 2.18, with the colours mixing at the overlaps to provide extra colours.

Seven colours are shown in Figure 2.18, but with all three light sources extinguished black is produced, and so a simple on/off RGB system is capable of producing eight colours (including black and white). An RGB monitor uses colour mixing in exactly the same way to give the pallette of eight colours. Where the intensity input is utilized it is possible to switch all the colours to half intensity. The number of colours

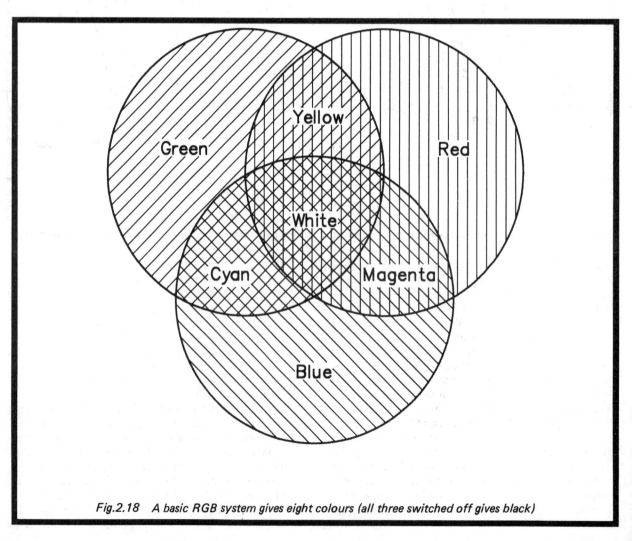

Fig.2.18   A basic RGB system gives eight colours (all three switched off gives black)

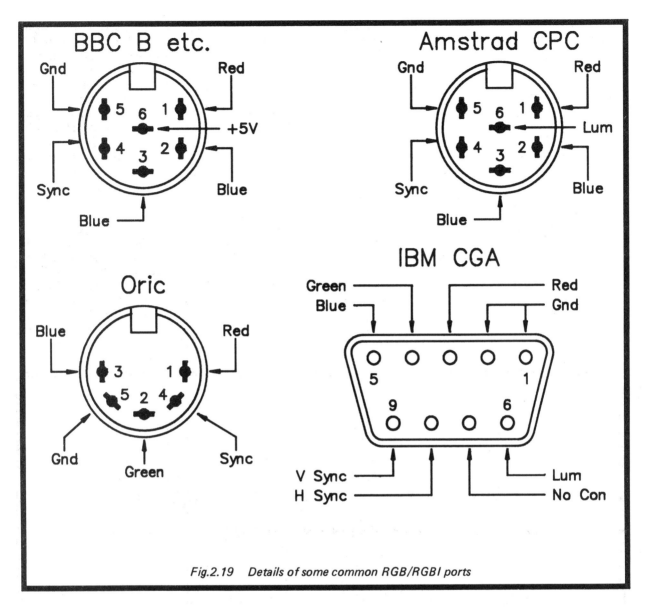

Fig.2.19   Details of some common RGB/RGBI ports

available from this RGBI (red, green, blue, intensity) system is often stated as being sixteen. However, half intensity black is presumably still black, and the number of colours available is actually only fifteen.

A lot of computers have RGBI outputs, including the BBC micros, the Electron, IBM PC/XT/AT computers fitted with the CGA (colour graphics adaptor) card, and the Amstrad CPC computers. Some have just the RGB outputs with no intensity output being implemented (the Oric computers for example). There are also computers which have the same colour pallette as RGB or RGBI monitors, but which provide their colour output in composite video form (some of the Commodore machines fall into this category). There is no difficulty in connecting an RGB or RGBI output to a monitor which has the appropriate type of input, and it is just a matter of connecting each terminal of the monitor's input socket to the corresponding terminals of the computer's monitor port.

The only slight problem is that a variety of connectors are used at both the computer and monitor ends of the system. A selection of RGBI input/output sockets are detailed in Figure 2.19. Some monitors are supplied with leads for connection to the 9 pin D connector of the IBM CGA card, and a short adaptor lead is then usually the easiest way of connecting them to a different type of computer.

Analogue RGB
For most purposes eight or fifteen colours are quite adequate, but for some applications a greater range of colours is preferable or even essential. Paint programmes that are limited to eight colours can be quite good fun, but do not really compare with programmes that can provide thousands of colours. The IBM EGA (enhanced graphics adaptor) and compatible display boards have a form of TTL output, but they have eight outputs plus an earth

terminal. Two of these outputs are separate vertical and horizontal synchronisation signals, and the other six are RGB outputs. Each colour has two outputs ("primary" and "secondary"), and with six logic outputs there are sixty-four different output combinations possible.

This gives the EGA display its pallette of sixty-four colours, but only sixteen of these can be displayed on the screen at any one time. This is not due to any deficiency in this method of interfacing or the monitor, both of which can provide all sixty-four colours on screen simultaneously. This limitation is imposed by the graphics adaptor card, or to be more precise, by its 256K of memory which can only map the 640 x 350 pixel display in sixteen colours. This arrangement of having more colours available than can be displayed at any one time is by no means unique to the EGA display, and is actually quite common with high resolution colour displays (as well as some medium resolution types). In some cases there are clever software tricks that can be used to take the number of on-screen colours beyond the official limit. The standard EGA connector is a 9 way D type, and it has the pin assignment shown in Figure 2.20.

Going beyond the EGA display with its sixty-four colours there are the displays that have analogue RGB outputs. Whereas a digital output only has two valid levels, an analogue signal can be varied continuously over its limits, and in theory anyway, has infinite

resolution. A monitor having analogue RGB inputs can therefore mix the three primary colours in any relative quantities to produce any desired colour. This is not to say that a computer which has analogue RGB outputs has an infinite range of colours and that they can all be displayed on screen at once. The circuits which drive the outputs are derived from digital circuits, and can only provide a limited number of steps.

The Commodore Amiga provides some 4096 colours by having sixteen different intensities for each of the three primary colours (16 x 16 x 16 = 4096), while the Atari ST has 512 available colours and presumably uses 8 intensities for each of the primary colours. Normally only about 16 of these colours are available at any one time, but both of them can use "tricks" to provide the full range of colours on-screen simultaneously (the "HAM" mode of the Amiga for example). Both of these computers, and other computers with similar capabilities (some of the VGA modes of the new IBM PS/2 computers for instance), can provide some really impressive results. They produce an almost photographic quality which does not seem to be achievable with computers that have similar resolutions but only a few colours available.

As far as interconnections are concerned, there are the three colour signals to be coupled from the computer to the monitor, plus an earth connection. It also seems to be the standard practice to have

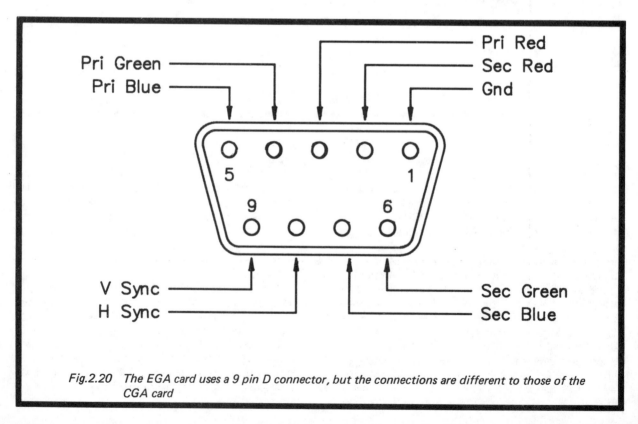

Fig.2.20   The EGA card uses a 9 pin D connector, but the connections are different to those of the CGA card

separate earth (or "ground") connections for the three colour signals in addition to an overall earth. This gives some four earth leads, plus possibly a fifth if there is also a separate earth for an audio input. I am not entirely sure why separate earths should be necessary, but this is usually done where there is a risk of a common earth causing stray coupling of one signal into another. Most analogue RGB systems seem to use a single synchronisation signal, but the VGA and MCGA systems seem to have separate vertical and horizontal synchronisation signals.

Analogue monitors and computers which have analogue outputs seem to use a variety of connectors. The popular NEC multisync II monitor has a standard CGA style 9 way D connector, but this operates in a variety of configurations depending on which of its operating modes is selected. A "multisync" monitor, incidentally, is one which can operate with a range of video standards, from standard RGB and RGBI to the more exotic ones which give higher resolutions and usually demand higher scanning rates (such as the EGA, VGA, and MCGA modes). Most multisync monitors will operate with both digital and analogue RGB signals, but the exact capabilities do seem to vary significantly from one monitor to another. If you need a multisync monitor for an unusual video mode it would be advisable to check that the particular one you are considering has the requisite inputs and scanning rate capability rather than just assuming that it does. Returning to the operating modes of the NEC multisync II, this table shows how each of its nine input terminals are allocated in each of its four operating modes.

apparently use a different method of connection. It is unfortunate that two standards have somehow arisen, but the method of connection shown in Figure 2.21 seems to be the most common one for computer equipment (and is the only one I have encountered).

Games Ports

A joystick port is something that can be found on most computers, and where it is absent there is usually a popular add-on that provides this function. The most common form of games port is the Atari/Commodore type, or a variation on this basic scheme of things. Figure 2.22 gives details of the Commodore 64 games port 1, which is a fully standard form of Atari/Commodore games port. Where a second games port is available (which it is on most computers including the Commodore 64) the second port uses what is essentially the same method of connection. However, pin 6 only functions as a firebutton on the second port, and it can not be used as an input for the lightpen.

There are two basic types of joystick: the switch and potentiometer varieties. The switch type indicates one of eight directions to the computer, and (usually) an on-screen object is moved in the direction indicated by the joystick. A potentiometer type is very different, and indicates a screen position to the computer. Usually, an on-screen object of some kind is moved to the indicated screen position. Atari/Commodore style games ports are intended for use with switch type joysticks.

The direction is indicated by four switches which connect to "JOYA0" to "JOYA3". These switches connect between their input terminals and the ground

Pin No.	CGA (TTL)	EGA (TTL)	PGC (ANAL)	VGA (ANAL)
1	GROUND	GROUND	RED	RED
2	GROUND	SEC RED	GREEN	GREEN
3	RED	PRI RED	BLUE	BLUE
4	GREEN	PRI GREEN	COMP SYNC	HOR SYNC
5	BLUE	PRI BLUE	MODE CONT	VERT SYNC
6	INTENSITY	SEC GREEN	RED GND	RED GND
7	NO CON	SEC BLUE	GREEN GND	GREEN GND
8	HOR SYNC	HOR SYNC	BLUE GND	BLUE GND
9	VERT SYNC	VERT SYNC	GND	GND

There is a standard connector for monitors, and this is the 21 way SCART type. This is to be found on some computer monitors (the Commodore 1081 for example), and should become more common as time passes. Details of the SCART connector are provided in Figure 2.21. Note that most monitors do not implement all these connections, and that the "data" and some of the audio terminals are usually just left unconnected. Also note that some monitors

terminal of the port (pin 8). They respectively give up, down, left, and right indications. Moving the stick (say) up and to the right will operate both the "up" and "right" switches, and will indicate that both upwards movement and movement to the right is needed. Thus the four switches can indicate a total of eight different directions. The "firebutton" input is wired to ground via the push-button switch of the joystick.

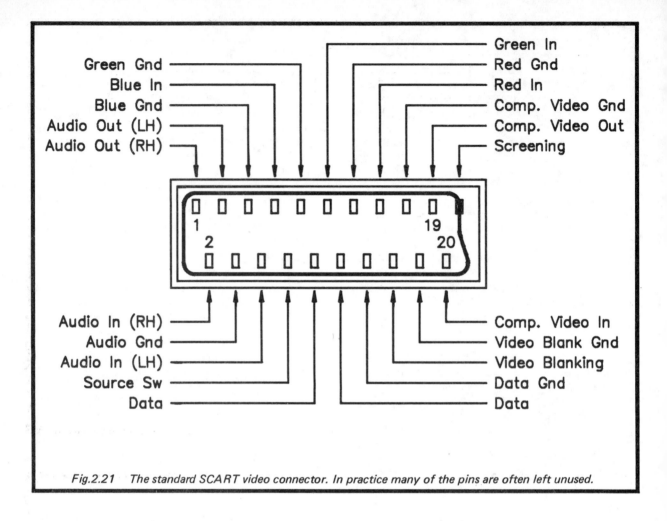

Green Gnd
Blue In
Blue Gnd
Audio Out (LH)
Audio Out (RH)

Green In
Red Gnd
Red In
Comp. Video Gnd
Comp. Video Out
Screening

1
2
19
20

Audio In (RH)
Audio Gnd
Audio In (LH)
Source Sw
Data

Comp. Video In
Video Blank Gnd
Video Blanking
Data Gnd
Data

Fig.2.21   The standard SCART video connector. In practice many of the pins are often left unused.

There are a few additional input terminals on the port, and these are for use with potentiometers. The two potentiometers connect from the +5 volt supply terminal to their respective inputs. I suppose that it would be feasible to use potentiometer joysticks with this type of games port by utilizing these two inputs, but they do not seem to be used this way in practice. They are primarily intended for use with games "paddles", which are effectively potentiometer joysticks which only provide side to side control. In fact this facility seems to be little used even for "paddles", and it appears to have been omitted altogether from some recent computers that have this style of games port (the Atari ST series of computers for instance).

There have been modified versions of this original form of the games port, of which the Atari ST version is just one example. Apart from omitting the paddle inputs, it has been modified to permit a mouse to be connected to port 1 (or "Port 0" as Atari have designated it). The games ports of the Commodore Amiga computers have been similarly modified, but still seem to retain the ability to take games "paddles". This is achieved by having many of the terminals serve more than one function. They can

both operate with standard Atari/Commodore style joysticks.

The Amstrad computers use a modified version of the standard arrangement which omits the "paddle" inputs but permits a single port to accommodate two joysticks. In fact this is not strictly correct, and only one joystick connects to the port. The second joystick plugs into a 9 way D plug fitted to the first joystick. Figure 2.23 provides details of the Amstrad style games port.

This follows the standard Atari/Commodore layout quite closely, and it should be possible to use a standard switch type joystick if only a single joystick is to be used. The "Common" input replaces the "GND" terminal of the standard games port, but it is used in precisely the same way. A standard switch type joystick might not be satisfactory if used with an Amstrad computer, since the Amstrad port has provision for a second "firebutton", which is absent from the standard switch type joystick. The second joystick is connected in the same way as the first apart from the fact that it uses the "COM2" terminal instead of the "Common" one.

Analogue joysticks seem to be used with few computers. They are the standard type for

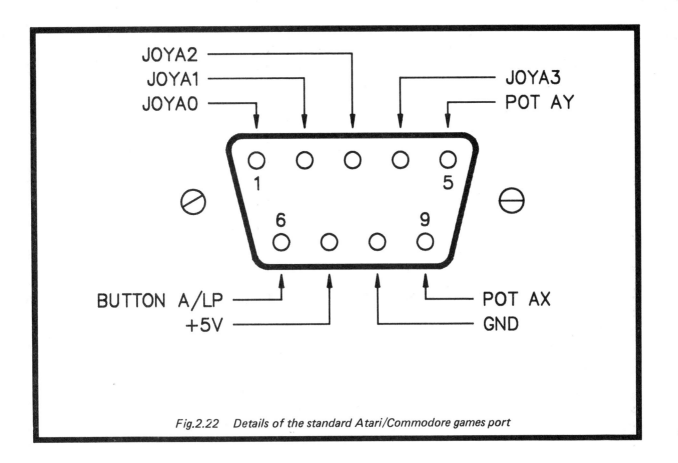

Fig.2.22   Details of the standard Atari/Commodore games port

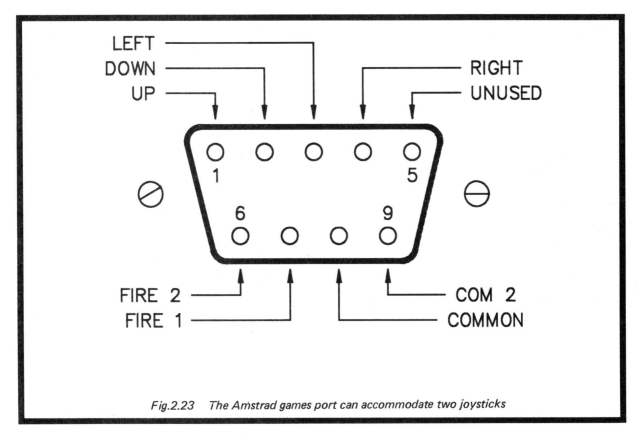

Fig.2.23   The Amstrad games port can accommodate two joysticks

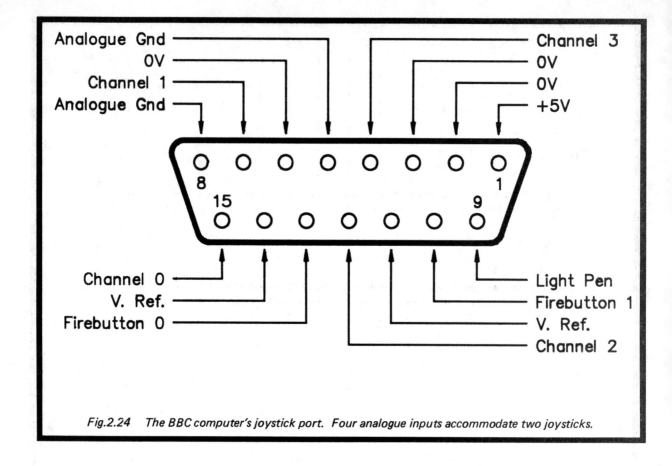

Analogue Gnd
0V
Channel 1
Analogue Gnd

Channel 3
0V
0V
+5V

8
15

1
9

Channel 0
V. Ref.
Firebutton 0

Light Pen
Firebutton 1
V. Ref.
Channel 2

Fig.2.24   The BBC computer's joystick port. Four analogue inputs accommodate two joysticks.

the IBM PC etc. and compatibles, but this type of controller does not seem to be in widespread use in the U.K. (probably due to the built-in switch type joystick interface on the popular Amstrad PCs). This type of joystick was used on the now obsolete Dragon computers, but they are probably most widely used in the U.K. with the **BBC** series of computers (apart from the model **A** which lacks the analogue input port). Figure 2.24 shows details of the BBC computer's analogue port, which uses a 15 way D type connector.

Unlike the "paddle" inputs of an Atari/Commodore games port, all three terminals of the potentiometer are used by the **BBC** port.

The track terminals connect across the 1.8 volt reference voltage and the analogue ground terminal (separate terminals are available for each joystick). The wiper terminal (which is usually the middle one of the three) connects to one of the analogue inputs ("Channel 0" to "Channel 3"). There are two inputs for each joystick so that each one can provide control in two planes. "PB0" and "PB1" are the "firebutton" inputs, and these are used in the same way as their equivalents on a switch type joystick.

Obviously switch type and analogue joysticks are totally incompatible, and you must use the right kind for the type of port fitted to your computer.

IEEE488

The IEEE488 interface (also called the "Hewlett Packard Instrument Bus" or something similar) is one of the less well known computer interfaces. It is mainly used for scientific instruments and other specialised pieces of equipment, although I believe it was used on some early Commodore machines for communications with peripherals such as disk drives. In fact it is still used on Commodore 8 bit machines such as the Commodore 64, but in considerably modified form. The standard IEEE488 interface uses a 24 way connector which is rather like a cut down Centronics type connector. The connector for the Commodore IEEE488 style interface is a 6 way DIN type. Connection details for these are provided in Figures 2.25 and 2.26.

The main difference between these two types of interface is that the full IEEE488 interface is a parallel type while the Commodore type is a form of serial interface. The two are therefore totally incompatible, although interface units to permit the Commodore 64 etc. with standard IEEE488 devices have been (and probably still are) available.

An important difference between these interfaces and most other types is that they provide two-way communications via a single wire (Commodore version) or an 8 bit parallel bus (standard IEEE488

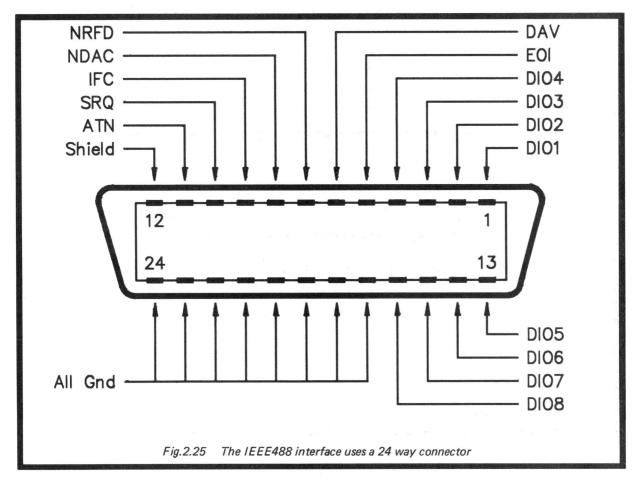

Fig.2.25   The IEEE488 interface uses a 24 way connector

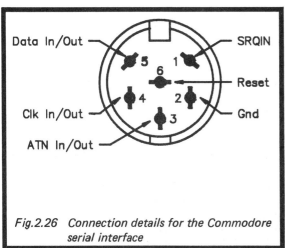

Fig.2.26   Connection details for the Commodore
serial interface

version). Devices that transmit on the data lines are "talkers", and those that receive on them are "listeners". A device does not have to be one or other of these, something like a disc drive will need to both send and receive data. Devices of this type are "talkers/listeners", but at any one time they can only provide one or other of these functions. This limitation is enforced by the single data wire or set of data wires. There is another category of IEEE488

device, and this is the "controller". For a system of this type to function properly it is essential to have a controlling device which ensures that only one device at a time is sending out data onto the data line or lines. The purpose of the "control" is to provide this supervision of the system, and it is almost invariably a computer or some form of dedicated microprocessor based controller.

The data lines actually carry more than just data being passed from one device to another, and they carry such things as "addresses" and status information. Addresses are important in a system of this type where there will usually be several "listeners", and it will often be necessary to direct information to just one of these at a time. Other lines are used for general control and handshaking. The DAV (data valid) line is used to indicate that valid data is present on the data lines (similar to the strobe line of a Centronics interface), while the EOI (end or identify) is used to show when the transfer of data has been completed. IFC (interface clear) is a sort of reset line that is used by the controller to initialise the system. The NDC (not data accepted) line is used by a "listener" to show that it is receiving data. SRQ is the service request line, and it is used by any device that wishes to gain the attention of the "controller". The ATN (attention) line is activated by the controller when it is placing an instruction onto the data lines (or data line in the case of the Commodore serial version).   The REN (remote enable) line is used to enable and disable the data bus.   The data bus is disabled when manual control of a device is required.   The sophisticated method of handshaking used in this system ensures that there are no difficulties with devices sending data more quickly than other devices can process it. The whole system is effectively slowed down to a rate that can be handled by the slowest unit in the system.

Obviously the Commodore serial version lacks many of the control lines, but this system still works in broadly the same way.   Being a serial system it tends to be much slower than the parallel version. Note that it is a synchronous system, with a clock signal rather than a standard baud rate to ensure proper synchronisation of the sending and receiving devices.

Chapter 3

LANGUAGES

Machine Code

Machine code is the native language of microprocessors. As explained in Chapter 1, each microprocessor has its own instruction set, though there are 'families' of devices using the same code. How difficult it is to learn machine code depends to some extent on which microprocessor you wish to program, however, in general, it is never easy.

Machine code consists entirely of numbers. Machine code programming involves writing programs directly in these numbers, or opcodes as they are called. It is difficult for humans to remember which number represents which operation, unless the number of operations available is very small. Also, it is only possible to tell which numbers represent instructions within a program, and which represent addresses or data, by their positions within the program. It is therefore very difficult to 'read' a pure machine code program.

Pure machine code programming is hardly ever done for the microprocessors used in home and small business computing, though it is done to a limited extent with the small microprocessors used in such things as washing machines. Sometimes a machine code program is written using the mnemonics for the instructions in the first place, and then is converted into machine code by looking up the opcodes corresponding to the mnemonics, but this is strictly a form of assembly language programming, hand assembling.

Assembly Language

Assembly language is the first step in changing the nature of computer programs from what the machine requires to what it is easy for humans to write and comprehend.

Assembly language is a method of writing machine code programs, but instead of having to deal directly with the machine opcodes, each operation is represented by a mnemonic, usually consisting of three letters, e.g. ADD, BEQ, JSR. The program is first written as a text file, using an editor or word processor, and is then passed through the assembler, which looks up the opcodes corresponding to the mnemonics, and thus forms the final machine code.

In fact a good assembler will do much more than this. Most will automatically calculate the displacements for branch instructions, so you need to know only where you want the program to branch, not how many bytes it is from the branch instruction. Often you can use labels for addresses, which makes the program easier to read as well as write. A good assembler will also accept data in either hex or decimal form, and often binary as well.

There are, however, less sophisticated assemblers, usually supplied as parts of machine code monitor programs, or as part of a high-level language (e.g. BASIC) interpreter.

The simplest assemblers are the direct or in-line type. These offer few facilities, and assemble each line as it is entered, putting the code directly into memory. They are usually found only as part of machine code monitor programs, and are used for experiment rather than for writing extensive programs. The code is usually assembled direct into memory then executed from the monitor. This type of assembler cannot usually calculate branch offsets, and does not allow the use of labels.

Similar assemblers are sometimes included in BASIC interpreters (the best known, perhaps, being the one in the BBC micro). These are mainly used to write short bits of assembly language programming as parts of BASIC programs, the code being assembled when the program is run, and then executed from within the BASIC, though they can be used to write stand-alone machine code. Calculation of branch offsets is usually possible with these assemblers.

The most efficient assemblers are of the two-pass type with separate editors. As the name suggests, the assembler makes two passes of the assembly language text file to generate the machine code program. This allows forward as well as backward branch offsets to be calculated. During the first pass, if the assembler finds any labels in branch instructions for which it has no address (which means they are further on in the program) it keeps a table of where the labels are referred to, and then during the second pass the actual address is inserted. (Some of the assemblers included in BASIC interpreters can be turned into two-pass types by putting the assembly language within a BASIC loop.)

Some assemblers for some microprocessors actually use a third pass, this being an optimising pass, changing some instructions to shorter forms giving more compact code or allowing faster execution where this is possible.

BASIC

BASIC is ubiquitous in computing. It is the language which is supplied as standard with the majority of microcomputers, and with home computers it is normally built-in on ROM, so that when you turn on the computer you go straight into the language. On such machines it can be difficult to separate BASIC from the operating system.

The name BASIC is an acronym, derived from Beginners All-purpose Symbolic Instruction Code (alternative derivations are to be found, but this is the generally accepted one). It was devised in its original form at Dartmouth College in the U.S.A.

BASIC is an interpreted language. This means it has the usual disadvantage of being rather slow. However, by comparison with other interpreted languages, the best BASICs are fast. As might be expected with such a popular language, there are many compilers for various versions of BASIC, including some of the versions supplied built-in to home computers, and also versions written specifically for compiling (some of which have interpreters for program testing!).

In BASIC variables are typed, which is to say they are defined as either numeric, representing numerical values on which mathematics can be performed, or string, which are simply strings of the characters which can be printed on the screen (including the numeric characters and special control characters). Functions are usually provided to convert strings of valid numeric characters to numeric form, and numeric values to string form. Numeric variables may be further typed into integer, real, double precision, and other types.

Large amounts of data, both string and numeric, can be handled by subscripted variables, commonly called arrays. In arrays, the individual variables are addressed by the variable name and one or more numeric values, the subscripts, representing the position of the variable in the array. As the numeric value(s) can be given as either constant or numeric, this allows easy programming to step through an array in sequence, or to access it randomly.

BASIC is a good number crunching language, and has full facilities for floating-point mathematics, and often for integer arithmetic as well (some early and primitive BASICs may be integer only). A wide range of mathematical and trigonometric functions are built-in, but the range provided does vary somewhat from dialect to dialect. There is almost invariably a facility provided to generate your own functions from combinations of the ones provided to obtain more advanced facilities. In some versions these *user-defined functions* are very sophisticated, and may be spread over several lines.

On the other hand, BASIC handles text, especially formatted text, rather clumsily. Storage in strings is not really adequate, and the string-handling functions rather limited.

Facilities for handling constant data within programs is also limited. Lists of data can be included in programs, and accessed sequentially, though in some versions, the RESTORE statement allows limited random access. In others it only allows you to start reading the data list again from the beginning. The only way to add constant data is to edit the program.

If variable data is to be saved from one running of a program to another, it must normally be explicitly saved to disc (or other non-volatile medium) by the program, and reloaded when the program is run again (in a few small home computers, saving the program also saves the variables). Advanced BASICs provided with or for computers intended for business use may include facilities for handling data files directly on disc, and in some cases these facilities can be very sophisticated (for example Locomotive Software's Mallard BASIC and BASIC 2).

The earliest BASICs date from the days when the usual output from a computer was on a teleprinter rather than a VDU screen. To make editing programs easier (or possible!) in this environment, the program lines were numbered, and were stored in memory, and (jumps and branches excluded) executed in the order of the line numbers. Line numbering has until very recently been an identifying feature of BASIC, as very few other languages use this feature. However, with VDUs for output, screen editing is possible and line numbers are not necessary, and on the latest versions they are optional, and are used simply as labels. The lines are stored as entered on the screen, not necessarily in the order of any numbering.

When first introduced, BASIC was rather a poorly-featured language. This was necessary because of the small amounts of memory available on the machines of that time. Decision making was in the form of IF . . . THEN statements which could test a condition and either continue execution in sequence if the test failed or branch to a specified line if true. Writing practical programs involved a fair amount of use of unconditional branches, the infamous 'GOTO'. This lead to BASIC getting the reputation of being an unstructured and untidy language.

When graphics and sound were first added to microcomputers there were at first no BASIC commands to control these, and such control was only possible either by direct memory addressing using PEEK and POKE, or by direct port addressing. Programs using a lot of graphics and sound could be very difficult to follow, consisting almost entirely of numbers, and little better than machine code. (The Commodore 64 BASIC was perhaps the most notorious in this respect.)

However, BASIC is very much a living language, and extra features have been added as new versions have been written, partly to improve the structure of the language, and partly to give easy access to all the graphics and sound capabilities of current machines. As a result of this, BASICs are now some of the most powerful languages around. Many modern BASICs have some or all of the following advanced features.

PROCEDURES. Instead of the subroutines of the early BASICs, modern versions allow the use of named procedures. Provided sensible names are chosen, these make program readability much better. Generally, you can also pass parameters to procedures, which means you can send data to them on which they are to work when calling them, just as you can with in-built commands.

MULTI-LINE IF . . . THEN STATEMENTS. As mentioned above, early BASICs only allowed branching after IF . . . THEN tests. The first improvement was to allow the execution of other statements conditionally, and then to allow a choice between two sets of statements by using IF . . . THEN . . . ELSE conditionals. More than one statement could be placed after THEN (and also after ELSE), but the whole statement had to be on one line. This could lead to very long untidy lines. Latest versions allow such conditionals to be spread over several lines. The block starts with the IF . . . THEN statement with the conditional test in it. It is followed by the statements to be executed if the condition is true. Optionally, there may then be the ELSE statement, followed by statements to be executed if the condition is false. The end of the block is indicated by a statement which is usually ENDIF.

MULTI-LINE USER-DEFINED FUNCTIONS. Most BASICs allow user-defined functions to evaluate expressions which are used often in a program. Usually such functions can contain only one expression, and can only be used to execute mathematical operations, not other statements such as PRINT. More powerful versions have user-defined functions which are procedure-like, which can be spread over several lines, and contain almost any statement in the language.

LOOP STRUCTURES. The first loop structure to be included in BASIC was the FOR . . . NEXT loop, which allowed the statements in the loop to be repeated a set number of times, a variable being used to count the repetitions and control the loop. Later, the REPEAT . . . UNTIL and WHILE . . . WEND loops were added. Both of these will continue to loop until a condition (like those used in IF . . . THEN statements) is true. In REPEAT loops the condition is at the end of the loop, in WHILE loops it is at the end. BASICs tended to have one or the other, but not both. The best modern versions do have both, or they may have them in the DO . . . LOOP form, which allows the condition to be placed at either end as required, i.e. DO WHILE . . . LOOP or DO . . . LOOP UNTIL.

You may have gathered that there are now considerable differences between different BASICs. Whilst this is certainly true, the incidences of one command word being used for two (or more) different purposes are fortunately quite few, and it is usually possible for a person who is familiar with one version of BASIC to program in another version, though frequent consultations of the manual are likely to be necessary!

BASIC remains very much a living (and growing) language. The latest versions allow full access to the graphics control environments (e.g. Digital Research's GEM), and as computer facilities grow, no doubt BASIC will grow with them. However, these advanced forms are now so comprehensive that they run the risk of being incomprehensible, and the claim of BASIC to be a beginner's language must in some cases be considered questionable.

Although BASIC has come in for a lot of criticism over the years, the best of the latest BASICs are extremely good in most respects. It is language that we have used for a wide range of applications — some quite mundane and others of a specialised scientific nature. BASIC must be rated as one of the most versatile of programming languages, unlike many programming languages that are highly specialised in their practical applications.

LOGO

LOGO was invented by Dr Seymour Pappert of MIT as a teaching language for beginners to programming, particularly young children. It is a highly structured language, which forces academic concepts of 'correct' programming technique on the user. LOGO is strictly an interpreted language, there are no compiled LOGOs, and such a thing would be contrary to the whole concept of the language, which is essentially interactive.

LOGO is best known for its 'turtle graphics' in which the 'turtle', which can be either a robot device or a 'virtual turtle' on the screen, moves around in response to such commands as "FORWARD 50" and "RIGHT 90", drawing line figures.

There is, however, much more to LOGO than this. It is one of the family of list processing languages, which means data is stored in the form of lists of 'words', and you can also have lists of lists, list of lists of lists, and so on. Lists can be manipulated in various ways to allow information to be extracted. LOGO can be a good second language for BASIC programmers, as the two are very different, and some things which are very complicated to program in BASIC are relatively straightforward in LOGO. One example of this is data pattern matching.

LOGO comes with a set of in-built commands called primitives. You use these primitives in combination to form procedures, which in effect add new commands to the language. The idea is that you can use the primitives and your procedures in very much the same way, thus extending the language to your needs. Having written procedures, you can then use these within other procedures to perform even more complex tasks. You do not so much write a LOGO program to do a job and then run it, as extend the language to give it the required capabilities, and then work interactively with the language from command mode, or 'top level' as it is called.

LOGO is not really intended as a number crunching language, and in-built mathematical functions are usually limited. The language can, of course, be extended to perform almost any arithmetic or mathematics you require, but this can take a lot of programming.

Variables are not typed in LOGO. Both numeric quantities and what would be strings in other languages are stored as words, which can be simple variables or elements of lists.

LOGO is a highly standardised language and there are far fewer dialects than there are in most other languages. The two main ones are MIT LOGO an LSCI LOGO. Of the minor variants, Edinburgh LOGO is used mostly in primary schools, and Open LOGO, devised by the Open University in the U.K., which presumably is used by the Open University. It isn't found anywhere else, though. There are few differences between the dialects, and once you have learned one it is relatively easy to adapt to another, and even to convert programs between dialects (a mug's game in BASIC).

C

C is a compiled language (apart from a few interpreters that are intended for debugging purposes), and some computer users seem to have gained the impression that the "C" name stems from the fact that it is Compiled. In fact it is a development of the "B" programming language. C has its origins in the 1960s when a team at Cambridge produced a language called CPL (Combined Programming Language), or BCPL (Basic Combined Programming Language) as the eventual and somewhat cut down version became known. BCPL is still around today incidentally, but does not seem to be used to any great extent. It was from BCPL that the B language was developed in the U.S.A. in 1970 by Ken Thompson. This was further developed into C by Dennis Ritchie of Bell Laboratories in 1972, and it was defined in the book "The C Programming Language" by Dennis Ritchie and Brian Kernighan. This book is also known as "The C Programmer's Bible", and it is generally considered to be essential reading for anyone who is going to undertake any major C programming.

C has become very popular, and it has a number of factors in its favour. As someone who has to work with several microcomputers, the ability to use the same language on several machines without having to adjust to changes in syntax etc. when changing machines is a highly attractive one. There is also the possibility of writing a program for one computer and then easily converting it for operation on several other computers, which has an obvious appeal to virtually any programmer. A lot of computer languages are supposedly very "portable", but few can genuinely produce portable programs. C is certainly an exception, and it is aided in this respect by the fact that it was quite rigidly defined at the outset. This has left little scope for authors of C compilers to do their own thing and introduce non-standard features. Of course, as with any programming language the portability of programs is dependent on add-ons to the language (such as graphics libraries) either not being used, or being available for any

computer on which the program must be run. Provided no add-ons of this type are used, C programs will usually run on other computers with little or no conversion being necessary.

C is not really a beginner's language. The brevity of its name is reflected in the program listings which are almost invariably cryptic in the extreme. I have heard it described as a high level language for low level programmers, and this seems a pretty apt description. It has some features which have parallels in assembly language, but it is a genuine high level language with string functions and the like. On the face of it, C should be easy for someone who has used BASIC plus assembly language routines, which means a good many home computer users. Not everyone with such a programming language finds C palatable though. A BASIC program line might be legal in C, but it might not provide the same function. You have to be prepared to learn C right from the beginning rather than trying to jump straight in and produce large programs. In C you have to declare variables, rather than simply inventing them as you go along, as in BASIC. This is no great problem as modern text editors make it easy to go back to the beginning of a program and add in any variables that are newly added. You have to get used to this way of doing things though, and be careful not to overlook any undeclared variables. The transition from BASIC to C could be difficult for someone who has become set in his or her ways. It is a type of language that is suitable for dabbling in if you are experienced in another language, and would like to try it out by producing a few simple programs.

Pointers are usually reckoned to be the most difficult aspect of C for beginners to grasp. Basically a pointer is just a variable that selects another variable. One use of this "indirection" is to enable one program module to operate with several sets of data, with the pointer or pointers being used to select the desired set. A more common use is to enable a program to easily access a character within a block of text, or something of this nature. This type of thing can only be undertaken in a relatively clumsy fashion using many programming languages.

Although C is not regarded by all as a structured language, it can be used for large and structured programs. It is not a structured program in the sense that it does not force the use of a highly structured approach. It is a very powerful and versatile language which enables you to tinker in an unstructured manner at a low level if that is what is called for. It was originally designed for writing operating systems and other "background" software, but it is used for a wide range of program types. It is well suited to small utility programs as well as large projects such as spreadsheets, databases, and word processors. It is much used by professional programmers, and is arguably the fastest programming language for microcomputers apart from assembly language/ machine code. Probably its main drawback is that it can be easy to make mistakes and difficult to debug the affected programs.

Pascal and Modula 2

Pascal was written to provide a programming language that would encourage good (structured) programming techniques, and it was designed by Professor Niklaus Wirth in the early seventies. A Pascal program generally takes the form of a main program having a series of conditional instructions, plus sub-programs (or whatever term you prefer) which the main program branches to. Of course, these days this is not exactly a unique feature, and a number of languages permit this structured approach.

Whereas C does little to disguise the way in which the computer stores and handles data, Pascal has a so-called "real-world" approach in which there are strict data types which can only be handled in ways in which the programming language considers to be valid. It is very logical in this respect, but possibly a little limiting. Of course, many languages have data types, but in Pascal the types can be precisely defined. If some variables will be integers in the range 0 to 100, then you can define a data type as integers in this range, and then use this data type for these variables. With most other languages you would select the nearest applicable data type from a list of predefined types. In our example above this would probably be a simple 8 bit number (0 to 255 in decimal terms), but you might have to use a multi-byte variable where a single byte would suffice.

Whereas C is rather cryptic, and following program listings can be difficult for even an experienced C programmer, Pascal listings are generally much easier to follow. You do not have to use long variable names etc., but this is the convention with Pascal programs. Of course, this improved readability is at the expense of more typing by the programmer.

Pascal is a good general purpose language which has been used to produce a great deal of high quality software. It is not without its drawbacks though. One of these is that it is relatively difficult to learn and to fully master. It is a rather fussy language which makes it difficult to use on a quick trial basis. It is a matter of doing some determined learning or not bothering at all! It lacks features compared to some other popular programming languages, and it relies heavily on external libraries to augment the basic language. This is not an uncommon way of handling things with modern programming languages, but these add-on libraries are perhaps more important with Pascal than is the case with some of its competitors. Stemming from the lack of features of the original language, a lot of "improved" variations have been produced. This makes Pascal less portable than some other languages, particularly C.

Pascal is intended for use with the structured "top-down" approach to programming. This is where you gradually work out the overall structure of a program, breaking it down into sections and sub-sections until it is at the stage where you can begin to write the code. The traditional BASIC approach is the "bottom-up" method, which is generally a less well planned "suck it and see" method. Top-down programming is often likened to washing your hands after going to the lavatory — everyone says they do it! What is often seen as a blunder in the design of Pascal is that the sub-program definitions have to be included in the source program, which would seem to make it necessary to plan programs from the top-down and write them from the bottom-up. I would presume that the idea is to have the program thoroughly worked out before starting to write it. There is then no problem in writing it with the procedure definitions in the source program. Not everyone gets on well with such in depth program planning, and the nature of some programming is to some extent experimental, where a certain amount of the "suck it and see" approach is necessary in order to gauge the feasibility of the project.

Modula 2 tends to be regarded as the successor to Pascal, although I doubt if dedicated Pascal programmers see it in this way. It was designed by Professor Niklaus Wirth, the creator of Pascal. It is designed to use separately compiled program modules — something which is not part of the original Pascal language, but which is present in some more recent implementations.

The idea behind Modula 2 is to provide a programming language that is analogous to the way computer and electronic hardware is designed. Modern electronics is based very much on integrated circuits which generate electrical signals, or take in electrical signals and process them to produce a modified output signal. Even circuits which do not exclusively use integrated circuits are still largely composed of electronic "building-blocks" which produce or process signals. This brings tremendous advantages for the electronics designer who does not need to design each circuit from scratch. By using integrated circuits and established circuit blocks it is possible to put together quite complex circuits in a reasonable amount of time. The main tasks of the electronics engineer are to design the overall system, to make sure all the blocks fit together properly, and to design any circuit blocks where existing circuits do not provide exactly the required function.

Software development has tended to lag some way behind hardware, and the idea of Modula 2 is to use program modules to permit large programs to be quickly and easily built up. Rather than hardware processing electrical signals, it is program modules processing data. New modules can be produced where existing ones are inappropriate. The modules are sometimes called "software chips". Due to its modular nature, Modula 2 is well suited to large projects where two or more programmers will undertake the work. By having rigid rules for input/output, the modules produced by different programmers can be guaranteed to operate properly together.

This description of Modula 2 is a bit simplistic, and in practice things are a little more difficult to fully master. For someone who has become an expert BASIC programmer the transition to Modula 2 could be a difficult one. For the Pascal programmer the transition should be relatively painless.

Being a relatively new programming language, some implementations lag well behind other popular programming languages in terms of sophistication and ease of use. Some recent versions are very good in both respects, but others tend to be difficult and cumbersome in use. I have a version of Modula 2 for a powerful 16 bit computer, but with its masses of files it is barely usable. Modula 2 is not particularly fast by compiled language standards, but again, some recent implementations are much better in this respect and comparable to most Cs.

The Rest

This covers the most popular languages for microcomputers, but there are a larger number of other languages in use. Some of these are rather specialised in nature, such as the artificial intelligence languages Lisp and Prolog, and their many mutations. These languages do not really meet most people's definition of "intelligence", and are not capable of original thought. The idea is to provide a set of rules so that the program can make an intelligent guess instead of having to be fed with explicit data in normal computer fashion. For example, the CAD program AutoCAD is written using Lisp (a list processing language), and it includes a clever hatching feature. You indicate a border area, and the computer fills it in with a predefined pattern of lines. This may not seem particularly revolutionary, but the AutoCAD hatching facility goes beyond this basic scheme of things. You can select objects that will define a border area, and can also include objects within that area. The program decides which objects constitute part of the border and which are within the border area. It then hatches inside the border, but avoids drawing over the selected objects within the border. You do not have to tell the program which is which — it makes up its own mind. This type of thing can certainly make programs much quicker and easier to use, and takes them a step forward in terms of sophistication. It is something that might become more common as programmers endeavour to make their products more powerful than those of the competition.

Another use of artificial intelligence is in expert systems. In fact this is probably their main use. One application of this type is in medical diagnosis, where an expert system can be used to effectively give a doctor of relatively little experience some of the expertise of a consultant. This type of system is basically a database. However, the "intelligence" is used to take a list of symptoms and other relevant information and give a list of possible ailments, indicating the relative likelihood of each one. The program is not using some form of magic formula to come up with the answers — it has to be meticulously fed with data by an expert, and it is using his or her experience to work out what are most likely to be the right answers. For the program to work well it must be correctly seeded with data by an expert.

Both these languages are available as commercial programs for some computers, and they are also available as public domain/shareware software for certain machines.

Forth is a language that seemed likely to become very popular at one time, but is something of a rarity these days. Apparently it was originally designed for the control of radio telescopes. It is well suited to other control applications though, and could potentially be used in a wide range of applications. It has been described as being as difficult to learn as assembler while having the operating speed of BASIC. This is something of an exaggeration, and it is generally very much faster than an interpreted BASIC. It is somewhat lower level language though, and as such it is that much more difficult to master. It is a threaded interpretive language rather than a truly compiled type, which helps to give it the speed edge over an interpreted language such as a (non-compiled) BASIC. In effect, the source program statements are stored in a semi-interpreted form so that they can be quickly turned into a fully executable form and run when the program is run. With fully compiled languages now so commonplace the speed of Forth is perhaps less impressive than it once was. Also, with computers generally having much larger memories these days, a range of compiled languages (which tend to require large amounts of memory) are now available for most machines.

Forth's main claim to fame is its dictionary of instructions. The user can define new commands and add them to the dictionary, and they are then treated just like the original command words. This gives a form of modular approach with parts of a program being defined as new command words which can then be used as and when required.

Forth is certainly a very versatile language, but many programmers simply prefer to use assembly language where speed is important, or BASIC where it is not. It is available commercially for a number of computers, and there are also shareware/public domain versions for some machines. It is an interesting language to try out, but its reverse Polish notation is rather back-to-front compared with conventional notation, and it could take some getting used to.

C++ is a language which seems to have gained a fair amount of attention recently. It is an extension of C which permits object orientation. This subject is sufficiently involved to defy quick and meaningful explanations, and an in-depth study of the subject would seem to be in order if you wish to gain a real understanding of this subject. Apparently C++ was inspired by a language of the 1960s called "SIMULA", which was intended for programming real-time simulations. Another language inspired by SIMULA is "Smalltalk", which was produced by Xerox Parc in the 1970s. The most notable feature of Smalltalk is its use of windows and mice, and it is generally regarded as having inspired the use of these in the Macintosh and subsequent WIMP computers/software. It does in fact have a number of novel features, and is a very interesting language. However, it is something of a rarity, and finding a full implementation of Smalltalk for your particular computer could prove to be difficult (or impossible).

Fortran is a language which exists in both compiled and interpreted forms, but is normally compiled. There is more than one version of this language, but "Fortran 77" is the "standard" version. It is aimed primarily at scientific and engineering applications. Unlike BASIC and Forth which are often used in these same areas of application, it is more specialised and is little used for any other purposes. It is almost certainly the best choice for the majority of scientific and engineering applications. Its main drawback is that there are few (if any) low cost versions of this language. Also, like many advanced high level languages, it is mainly used on 16-bit systems rather than 8-bit types.

Chapter 4

NUMBERING SYSTEMS

The numbering system we use in everyday life is, of course, the decimal system, or "denary" system as it is alternatively known. This method of numbering is based on the number 10, but it is quite possible to have a system based on any number. There is normally no point in doing so, and the old imperial measures which were based on a variety of numbers (twelve in the case of feet and inches for example) are now well on the way to being phased-out in favour of the metric system. Truly "metricated" computers seem to be some way off, and for the foreseeable future they will work in binary.

Binary Numbers

I suppose that binary could reasonably be regarded as the simplest possible method of numbering. It is based on the number two, and where in the decimal numbering system the single digit numbers are from 0 to 9, in binary they are only from 0 to 1. In other words, the only valid number for each digit is 0 or 1, and absolutely nothing else is allowed! This might seem to be a pointless way of handling numbers, but it is very convenient from the hardware point of view. Representing just two numbers by an electrical signal is very easy. A low voltage (normally about 2 volts or less) is used to represent a 0, and a higher voltage (usually about 3 to 5 volts) represents a 1. These signal levels are often called "low" and "high" respectively, or "logic 0" and "logic 1". Although convenient for the hardware producers, this system has its limitations and drawbacks. There have been suggestions over the years that circuits which can work directly in decimal will be a practical proposition for widespread use before too long, but there seems to be little real prospect of such a development in the near future. For the time being circuits which work in binary are the only practical ones for general use.

Binary is easier to understand if you first analyse what an ordinary decimal number represents. If we consider the decimal number 238 for instance, the eight represents eight units (10 to the power of 0), the 3 represents three tens (10 to the power of 1), and the 2 represents two hundreds (10 to the power of 2). Things are similar with a binary number such as 1101. Working from left to right again, the columns of numbers respectively represent the units (2 to the power of 0), the 2s (2 to the power of 1), the 4s (2 to the power of 2), the 8s (2 to the power of 3), and so on. 1101 in binary is therefore equivalent to 13 in decimal (1 + 0 + 4 + 8 = 13).

It takes a lot of binary digits to represent numbers of quite modest magnitude, but this is the price that has to be paid for the convenience of simple binary hardware. A binary digit is normally contracted to the term "bit". One bit on its own is of limited value,

and bits are normally used in groups of eight, or multiples of eight. A group of eight bits is normally termed a "byte". A byte can only handle numbers from 0 to 255 (decimal). This is adequate for some purposes, but often larger values must be handled. A 16 bit binary number is usually termed a "word", and this gives a range of 0 to 65535 (decimal). 32 bits gives a range of 0 to something over four thousand million, which should be adequate for most purposes. A 32 bit number is normally termed a "long word".

You can not do much computing without coming across the term "k". This is the abbreviation for "kilobyte", which is a thousand bytes. In fact, to be precise, it is 1024 bytes. This may seem to be an odd number to choose, but a 10 bit binary number covers a range of 0 to 1023, or 1024 different values in other words. The extra 24 on each k is often not of great significance, but it is interesting to note that a computer with a "megabyte" of memory has 1048576 bytes of memory. Not a million bytes, and some 47k to 48k above the million byte mark. A "megabyte", which is often abbreviated to just "M", is the usual unit of measurement for large amounts of data, **RAM**, or whatever.

This table shows the number represented by bits in 16 bit numbers, and this might help to clarify the way in which the binary system operates. The numbers in the table are the ones that the bits represent when a 1 is present in that column of the binary number. If there is a 0 in a column, then that column always contributes 0 to the value of the number. We are using the convention of calling the units column bit 0, running through to bit 15 for the left-most column (not bits 1 to 16). The units column is often called the "least significant bit", or "LSB" for short. Bit 31 (or the left-most column that is actually used) is termed the "most significant bit", or just "MSB".

Bit	Decimal Value	Bit	Decimal Value
0	1	8	256
1	2	9	512
2	4	10	1024
3	8	11	2048
4	16	12	4096
5	32	13	8192
6	64	14	16384
7	128	15	32768

Addition of two binary numbers is a straightforward process which is really more simple than decimal addition. Here is a simple example of binary addition.

First number	240	11110000
Second number	85	01010101
Answer	325	101000101

As with decimal addition, start with the units column and work towards the final column on the left. In this case there is a 1 and a 0 in the units column, giving a 1 in the units column of the answer. In the next column two 0s give a 0 in the answer, and the next two columns are equally straightforward. In the fifth column there are two 1s to be added, giving a total of 2. Of course, in binary the figure 2 does not exist, and this should really be thought of as 10 (one 2 and no units), and it is treated in the same way as 10 in decimal addition. The 0 is placed in the answer, and the 1 is carried forward. In the seventh column this gives a total of 3 in decimal, but in this binary calculation it must be thought of as the binary number 11 (one 2 and one unit). Therefore, 1 is placed in the answer and 1 is carried forward. In the eighth column this gives an answer of 10, and as there are no further columns to be added, both digits are placed in the answer.

Signed Binary

The binary system described so far, which is often called "direct binary", is inadequate for many practical purposes. Its main drawback is that it can not handle negative numbers. Obviously you can simply add a minus sign ahead of a binary number to indicate that it is a negative number, but you have to bear in mind that for computer applications this is not valid. There is logic 0 and logic 1, but no logic − level!

One way around the problem is to use "signed binary". With a signed binary number the first bit is used to denote whether the number is positive or negative. The convention is for the first bit to be a 0 for positive numbers and a 1 for negative numbers. With this system the normal 8 bit range of 0 to 255 is replaced with a range of −127 to +127 (11111111 to 01111111). The problem is solved at the expense of decreased maximum magnitude for a given number of bits. Note though, that where two or more bytes (or words or long words) are used together to form a large number, only the most significant bit of the most significant byte needs to be used to indicate the sign of the number. It is not necessary to sacrifice the most significant bit of each byte to this task.

Obviously a certain amount of care needs to be exercised when dealing with binary numbers, and you must know whether you are dealing with direct or signed binary numbers. For instance, 10000001 could be 129 (direct binary) or −1 (signed binary). I have encountered computers which have a binary to decimal conversion facility, and which seem to get confused in this way. Results were as expected for answers up to 32767, but things went completely wrong with high numbers. This happens where the

computer operates with binary numbers of up to 16 bits in length, and it interprets any values it is fed as signed binary. This works fine if you know that it is working with signed binary. It also works fine if it is fed with binary values of 15 bits in length or less. The leading zeros then inform the computer that the number is a positive one, and the right answer is obtained. For numbers of more than 32767 the most significant bit is a 1, telling the computer that it is a negative number, even if you require a direct binary conversion.

In this basic form the signed binary system has its limitations. The problem is that although it can represent a wide range of positive and negative values perfectly adequately, calculations on simple signed binary numbers do not give the correct result. This is of only academic importance to users of high level applications programs and applications software. You give the computer such numeric data, positive, negative, or a mixture of the two, and everything is sorted out for you. It is something that is of greater importance to the low level (assembly language or machine code) programmer. Confusing results can be obtained unless you understand just how the microprocessor is handling things.

Ones Complement

The simple calculation shown below illustrates the problem that occurs using simple signed binary.

First number	16	00010000
Second number	−5	10000101
Answer	−21	10010101

Adding 16 to −5 should obviously give an answer of 11 and not −21. What is happening is that the negative sign of the −5 is being added to the answer so that the answer must always be negative if one of the numbers being added is a negative type. This is clearly incorrect, as in this example. The main bodies of the numbers are simply added together, and their signs are ignored. Negative values therefore increment the figure in the answer rather than decrementing it.

An alternative and related method of handling binary numbers is the "ones complement system". Here a negative number is the complement of its positive equivalent. For example, 16 is 00010000 in binary, and so −16 is 11101111 in ones complement binary. In other words, the 0s are simply changed to 1s and the 1s are changed to 0s. This gives much better results when used in calculations, as demonstrated by the example given below.

First number	16	00010000
Second number	−5	11111010
Answer	266	100001010

I suppose that on the face of it this answer is even further from the right answer than when simple signed binary was used. The margin of error is certainly much greater, but the usefulness of this system depends on how the answer is interpreted. The first point to note is that the positive number starts with a 0 while the negative number has a 1 as the first digit. Provided sufficient digits are used this will always be the case, and in this respect the ones complement system is the same as straightforward signed binary. The answer is completely wrong of course, but if the carry is ignored the answer is much closer to the right one. The answer is then 1010 in binary, or ten if converted to decimal. This is just one away from the right answer. So what happens if we try another example and ignore the carry.

First number	32	00100000
Second number	−4	11111011
Answer	27	00011011

As before, the answer is wrong but it is just one less than the right answer (which is of course 28 in this case).

Twos Complement

Clearly this system can be made to operate correctly, and it is just a matter of finding some way of correcting the minor error in the answer. The standard method used with most microprocessors is called "twos complement". This differs from ones complement in that once the complement of a number has been produced, one is added to it. Therefore, rather than −5 being represented as 11111010, it becomes 11111011 in twos complement. If we now apply this to one of the examples given earlier we obtain the following result.

First number	16	00010000
Second number	−5	11111011
Answer	11	00001011

This time, provided we ignore the carry, we do indeed obtain the correct answer of 11. This is a convenient way of handling subtraction (for microprocessors if not for humans), since subtraction can be carried out by the same circuit that handles addition. To handle a calculation such as 45 − 25 the value of 25 is converted to twos complement and then added to 45. In other words, instead of handling this calculation in the form 45 − 25 it is undertaken in the form 45 + (−25), and either way the answer is 20.

The following table shows some sample numbers in twos complement form, and this should help to clarify the system for you. Note that, like ordinary signed binary, the first digit is used to indicate whether the number is positive or negative.

Number	Positive	Negative
0	00000000	00000000
1	00000001	11111111
2	00000010	11111110
3	00000011	11111101
4	00000100	11111100
32	00100000	11100000
126	01111110	10000010
127	01111111	10000001
128	010000000	10000000

Note that with 8 bit twos complement numbers the range is from −127 to +128 (not −127 to +127 as with simple signed binary).

So far we have only considered calculations where the answer is a positive quantity, but the twos complement system works equally well if the answer is negative. This point is demonstrated by the example provided below.

First number	16	00010000
Second number	−31	11100001
Answer	−15	11110001

The twos complement system also functions properly when the two numbers being added are both negative, as in this example.

First number	−4	11111100
Second number	−8	11111000
Answer	−12	11110100

Binary Coded Decimal

Several microprocessors can operate using another form of binary called "binary coded decimal", or just "BCD". This is a somewhat less compact and efficient form of binary, it is generally somewhat slower, and it is not used in most applications. It does have its advantages though, and the main one is that it can be used to provide a very high degree of precision.

With BCD four binary bits (often termed a "nibble") are used to represent each decimal digit. The system operates in the manner shown below.

Decimal Number	Binary Code
0	0000
1	0001
2	0010
3	0011
4	0100
5	0101
6	0110
7	0111
8	1000
9	1001

The binary number is in fact just the ordinary binary bit code for the number concerned, and it is only for numbers of more than 9 that the system is different. The binary codes from 1010 to 1111 are unused, and all two digit decimal numbers require 8 bit BCD codes. For instance, the decimal number 64 would be represented by the 8 bit BCD code 01100100. The first four bits (0110) represent the six, and the second four bits (0100) represent the four. Each byte can therefore represent any two digit decimal number from 0 to 99, which compares to a range of 0 to 255 for an ordinary 8 bit binary number. This helps to contribute to the relative inefficiency of the BCD system. Of course, when a nibble is incremented by 1 from a value of 1001 (9 in decimal) it does not go to 1010 (which is an illegal code in BCD), but cycles back to 0000. A carry forward of 1 should then be taken to the next BCD nibble.

With this system there is no difficulty in handling large numbers, and it is just a matter of using several bytes in order to accommodate the required number of digits. Negative numbers and decimal points can also be handled with ease by this system, but this requires several additional bits. This information is usually carried in the most significant bits (i.e. the left hand end of the number). Some microprocessors perform BCD calculations by performing calculations in ordinary binary and then adjusting the result, but some have a true BCD operating mode.

Hexadecimal

Hexadecimal is a numbering system that you are almost certain to encounter a good deal. It is usually called by its abbreviated name of "hex". A problem with binary numbers is that they tend to have many digits with each one being a 0 or a 1, which makes them rather difficult to deal with in many circumstances. For instance, dealing with 16 or 24 bit addresses or microprocessor instruction codes in their binary form would probably be beyond most peoples' ability. On the other hand, binary numbers give a graphic representation of each bit in the register of a microprocessor, control register of a peripheral chip, output terminals of a printer port, or whatever. This is something that is often important, especially when dealing directly with the peripheral chips of a computer. Decimal numbers are much easier to deal with in that they are much shorter and are in a more familiar form. Unfortunately, a decimal number does not give much idea of the state of each bit in its binary equivalent. Converting a decimal number to its binary equivalent is not a particularly quick or easy process (without the aid of some computerised help anyway). Decimal numbers are consequently rather inconvenient when things must be visualised on a bit by bit basis.

The hexadecimal system gives the best of both worlds in that it takes just a few digits to represent even quite large numbers, and it is in fact slightly better than the decimal numbering system in this respect. On the other hand, it is quite easy to convert hexadecimal numbers to their binary equivalents when the state of each bit must be known. The conversion process is quite simple even with very large numbers. The hexadecimal system is based on the number 16, and there are sixteen single digit numbers. Obviously the numbers we normally use in the decimal system are inadequate for hexadecimal as there are six too few of them. This problem is overcome by augmenting them with the first six digits of the alphabet (A to F). It is from this that the system derives its name. The table given below helps to explain the way in which the hexadecimal system operates.

Decimal	Hexadecimal	Binary
0	0	0000
1	1	0001
2	2	0010
3	3	0011
4	4	0100
5	5	0101
6	6	0110
7	7	0111
8	8	1000
9	9	1001
10	A	1010
11	B	1011
12	C	1100
13	D	1101
14	E	1110
15	F	1111
16	10	10000
17	11	10001
18	12	10010
163	A3	10100011

What makes hexadecimal so convenient is the ease with which multi-digit numbers can be converted into binary equivalents. The reason for this is that each hexadecimal digit represents four binary bits. Take the hexadecimal number A3 in the above table for example. The digit A represents 1010 in binary, and the digit 3 converts to 0011. A3 therefore represents 10100011 in binary. You may find that you can memorise each of the sixteen four bit binary codes represented by hexadecimal digits, but a little mental arithmetic is all that is needed in order to make the conversion if you can not.

The digits in a hexadecimal number represent, working from left to right, the number of units, 16s, 256s, 4096s, 65536s, 1048576s, and 268435450s (approx.). You are unlikely to use hexadecimal numbers of more than eight digits in length, and mostly you will probably only deal with hexadecimal numbers having four digits or less.

Octal

Although the octal numbering system was much used in computer circles at one time, it seems to have fallen from favour. Hexadecimal now seems to have superseded it. As its name suggests, it is based on the number 8. The columns of figures therefore represent the units, 8s, 64s, 512s, 4096s, 32768s, etc. Only the first eight digits (0 to 7) of the decimal numbering system are utilised by the octal system, and so neither 8 or 9 are legal characters in octal.

In common with hexadecimal, octal helps to keep the number of digits in large numbers down to reasonable proportions, but it can easily be converted into binary if the state of each bit must be known. Whereas each hexadecimal digit represents a four bit binary code, each octal digit represents just three binary bits. With modern computing being based on 8 bit bytes, or multiples of eight bits, the three bit octal codes are less than totally convenient. It is probably this factor that has led to its decline in favour of the hexadecimal system. Here is a list of octal digits and the three bit binary codes that they represent.

Octal Digit	Binary Code
0	000
1	001
2	010
3	011
4	100
5	101
6	110
7	111

As with hexadecimal digits, the binary codes they represent are just the standard codes for the numbers concerned. It is probably not worthwhile taking the time to familiarise yourself with the octal numbering system as it is rarely if ever encountered in practice these days.

Conversions

Conversion from hexadecimal to binary is, as we have already seen, fairly straightforward. With a little experience a little mental arithmetic is all that is needed to make this type of conversion. Conversion in the opposite direction is equally simple. It is just a matter of breaking down the binary number into four bit groups and then converting each group to its corresponding hexadecimal digit.

Conversions that involve decimal numbers are a little more difficult to deal with. The easy way of handling the problem is to use a computer to make the conversion. Most BASICs can provide a hexadecimal to decimal conversion. If the computer accepts hexadecimal numbers with (say) a "&H" prefix to indicate that they are in hexadecimal, then giving the instruction:

PRINT &HXXXX RETURN

where "XXXX" is the hexadecimal number to be converted, should result in the decimal equivalent being printed on the screen. A conversion in the opposite direction might also be possible, and this is most commonly found in the form of a HEX$ function. You may even find that decimal to octal conversion is possible using an OCT$ function (as in Amiga BASIC for instance), although these days such a function would seem to be of largely academic interest.

Bitwise Operations

In computing numbers are not only manipulated using the normal mathematical functions. There are also the "bitwise" operations called "AND", "OR", and "XOR". These compare two binary numbers (literally) bit-by-bit, and the answer produced depends on the combination of 0s and 1s present in each column. ANDing produces a 1 in the answer only if there is a 1 in that column of both the numbers being ANDed. In other words, if a bit is set to 1 in the first number and the second, a 1 is placed in that bit of the answer. Hence the "AND" name of this logic operation. Here is a simple AND example.

First number	15	00001111
Second number	243	11110011
Answer	3	00000011

The answers obtained from bitwise operations can tend to look a bit random unless you consider what is happening on a bit by bit basis. A common use of the bitwise AND function is when less than all eight bits of a byte must be read. For instance, assume that we wish to know the state of bit 3 of a register in a peripheral device. Most computer systems do not provide any means of reading just bit of memory or peripheral devices. One way around the problem is to use a bitwise AND operation to mask off the unwanted bits. In this case bit 3 represents eight when it is set to logic 1, and so the masking number to use is eight (00000100 in binary). In the answer all the bits except bit 3 must be set to zero, as there is no way they can be set to 1 in both numbers. The situation is different for bit 3, where both bits could be at logic 1 if the second number also has this bit set to 1. The answer therefore reflects the state of bit 3 in the second number, and is eight if this bit is high, or zero if it is at logic 0. The ANDing provides the desired function with, in effect, only the required bit being read. It is possible to read more than one bit if desired. Just set any bits which must be read to logic 1 in the masking number — set any bits which must be masked off to logic 0 in the masking number.

Bitwise ORing is a similar process to ANDing, but a 1 is placed in a bit of the answer if there is a 1 in that bit of the first number, or the second number, or both. XORing differs from ORing in that it will place a 1 in a bit of the answer if there is a 1 in that bit of the first number or the second, but not if there is a 1 in both bits of these numbers. A common use of these bitwise operations (and the AND function) is in computer graphics. They are often used to ensure that the desired effect is obtained where one on-screen object overlaps another.

Note that many BASICs have AND and OR functions, but these can not always be made to operate in a bitwise manner. These bitwise operations should always be available at machine code level though.

OPERATING SYSTEMS

An operating system is one of those things that almost defies description. Practically every computer has what could be described as an operating system, and practically every time you get a computer to do something, however trivial, you are almost certainly making use of the operating system (even if only in an indirect manner). With a lot of home computers, when you switch on the machine it loads and runs its BASIC interpreter. With a computer of this type the operating system is largely hidden from the user, and it may be virtually inseparable from the BASIC interpreter program.

The operating system is usually more obvious with business computers where you are normally "in" the operating system once the computer has gone through its initial start-up and checking procedure. Some business computers are set up as "turnkey" systems, where they automatically run an applications program after the initial testing routine has been completed. In fact a system of this type still goes into the operating system after the initial checking routine, but the operating system is set up so that it automatically runs the applications program. Although the user may not be aware of it, the applications program will almost certainly make extensive use of the operating system.

Purpose

So just what is the purpose of an operating system? Its main function is to provide a set of routines to control input and output. In most cases any form of input or output is via the operating system, which means such things as the keyboard and the monitor screen as well as printer and serial ports. In other words, it provides a link between the microprocessor at the heart of the computer, and the various peripheral devices that connect it to the outside world. We are not talking here about physical links, but of software routines that control everything. These routines are usually available to the user via commands typed from the keyboard, so that tasks such as copying discs or printing out a disc file can be undertaken. They can also be accessed by applications programmers. It is not usually obligatory to access the peripheral chips via the operating system, but it is a convenient way of handling input and output. Why bother to write routines to control the peripheral devices when they are already there in the operating system just waiting to be used? Well, there is one reason which is speed. Where an application demands speed and the operating system proves to be inadequate in this respect, most programmers simply access the peripheral devices directly in an attempt to improve matters.

This is not necessarily something that is of purely academic importance. A purpose of many operating systems (including CP/M and MS-DOS) is to provide a standard input/output interface for applications programs. In other words, although two computers might have substantial differences in their hardware, provided they have the same operating system, an applications program designed to operate under that system should work equally well on either computer. In effect, where necessary the operating system software will disguise one piece of hardware to make it appear to operate like another (and similar) piece of hardware. It is this type of manipulation that can tend to slow down an operating system. If an applications programmer writes a program to directly access the input/output chips, assumptions have to be made about which chips the computer will use, and where they will appear in the input/output map. In practice this means that the program becomes "machine specific", and is unlikely to run on any other computer even if it is running under the appropriate operating system. The practical result of this is that computers designed for one of the popular operating systems do not just use the same microprocessor as other machines designed for that operating system, but all their hardware is usually very much the same. The best example of this is the IBM PC and its derivatives such as the AT. There are countless IBM PC compatibles in existence, most of which are the same basic design as the original, albeit in somewhat disguised form in the majority of cases.

Using an Operating System

There are several operating systems in common use these days, and although they have many differences, they also have a number of features in common. When you are "in" an operating system there is normally a "prompt" to indicate that the computer is ready and waiting for a typed command. This is often a ">" symbol, but others are used and there may be several options. Often the prompt is preceded by a letter to indicate which disc drive you are "in". All this means is that unless you specify a particular drive, or other input/output device, the computer will assume that the current drive is the one that should be used as the source for input or the destination of any output. The drives are usually named "A", "B", "C", etc., but other methods of identification are also used. For instance, in AmigaDOS the drives are called "DF0", DF1", etc. ("DF" presumably standing for "drive-floppy").

Most modern operating systems permit the disc drive of a single drive system to operate as both drive

"A" and drive "B". This is not always possible, and it is not a feature of CP/M prior to CP/M version 3.0 (or "CP/M Plus" as it is often called). A lack of this facility limits the usefulness of a single drive system as there may be no way of copying disc files or backing-up complete discs. Where it is permitted, how can one drive act as two? Nothing particularly clever is needed in order to achieve this, and it is just a matter of the drive acting first as drive "A", then as drive "B", then as drive "A" again, and so on. This is not quite as good as having two drives as a large amount of disc swapping can be needed. Some programs are unusable on a single drive system as they would require an inordinate amount of disc swapping.

AmigaDOS does not allow one disc drive to act as two, but it still permits disc copying and similar functions to be carried out without any difficulty. There is more than one way of achieving this type of thing, but the usual AmigaDOS method is to use discs as logical devices. The precise way in which logical devices are treated varies from one operating system to another, and AmigaDOS is rather more advanced than many in this respect. The general idea of logical devices is to have a number of notional devices (the logical devices), and the actual (physical input/output) devices of the computer. Usually it is possible to assign logical devices to actual devices. For instance, "PRN" might be the notional printer device, and by assigning this to the second serial port, this port would effectively be made the printer port. The usual way of identifying logical devices is to use a colon (:) at the end of the device name.

If AmigaDOS encounters a logical device name that is not one of its normal devices (such as the keyboard, printer port, etc.) it assumes that this device is a disc. I do not mean that it assumes this device to be a disc drive — I mean it assumes it is a floppy disc. Many operating systems permit "labelling" of discs, where the disc is given a name which is actually stored on the disc. In most cases though, this is not of any great significance, and its purpose is much the same as a paper label stuck on a disc for identification purposes. With some operating systems, including AmigaDOS, the naming of discs is of greater importance. If you wish to (say) copy a file from one disc to another, you can use the name of the source disc (complete with colon) followed by the file name, and the name of the destination disc (again complete with colon). The computer then knows precisely what it must do, and it then tells you when to place which disc in which disc drive. If the system only has a single drive, then this drive will always be used for any reading from or writing to disc. This method can seem to be a little fussy and awkward when compared to systems which simply use one drive as drives "A" and "B". It certainly needs a certain amount of planning in that it only works properly if you name each disc before starting to use it. It is really a very advanced and versatile way of handling

things, and is especially good for those with single drive systems.

The Commands

An operating system can be used to perform a variety of input/output related tasks, but just what are these tasks? The exact facilities available varies considerably from one operating system to another, but basic ones such as disc copying and formatting should be available on any operating system. In the section that follows this there is an alphabetical list of MS-DOS commands, together with a brief explanation of each one. Some of the more obscure commands which defy brief explanation have been omitted. This list gives a good idea of the types of task that can be undertaken using a typical operating system. With most operating systems there are two basic varieties of command; "internal" commands and the "external" type. An internal command is one that is loaded into the computer's memory when the operating system is "booted". Internal commands are therefore available at any time. The frequently used commands such as "copy" are mostly of the internal type. An external command is one which is stored on disc, and which is consequently only available if that disc can be accessed by the computer.

An obvious omission from the list of commands is one to run application programs. With MS-DOS, and most other operating systems, it is merely necessary to type the name of the program and press the "RETURN" key in order to run an applications program, and there is no "RUN" command as such.

Assign

Assign is used to assign a different drive letter to a disc drive. This is mainly used where an applications program does not let you use the drive or drives you wish to use. With the assign command you can get such a program to use one disc drive while it thinks it is using a different one.

Attrib

This command sets or resets the read only attribute of a file, or it can be used to display the current state of this attribute. Discs can be write protected via their write protect tab, but most operating systems also allow for software write protection of discs, or in some cases (including MS-DOS) individual files can be write protected.

Backup

Backup is used to make backup copies of discs as insurance against the original becoming lost or damaged. In practice it is mainly used with hard disc machines to backup the hard disc onto a number of floppy discs.

Break

It is possible to break out of some operating system activities (even from within applications programs) by pressing the "CONTROL" and "C" keys. Normally the operating system only checks for this break sequence when reading the keyboard, or writing to the screen or printer. The break command can be used to extend the break sequence to other activities such as reading from and writing to discs.

Chdir

Chdir is an abbreviation for "change directory". In fact MS-DOS accepts the further abbreviation of "cd". Directories and sub-directories are mainly used with hard discs, although they can (and sometimes are) used with floppy discs. Directories and sub-directories divide a disc into what are effectively separate compartments. If, for example, a computer is to be used to run a spreadsheet, a word processor, and database program, these could each be given their own directories. Initially the operating system is in what is called the "root" directory, and the directories for the three programs would really be sub-directories of the root directory. However, the convention is for sub-directories of the root directory to be called directories. Sub-directories of these directories are called sub-directories, as are any sub-directories of the sub-directories (they are not called sub-sub-directories). You can have a large number of sub-directories if desired, and this is often a convenient way of doing things. For instance, the three programs could each have a separate sub-directory for each month's data. This would make it relatively easy to track down a required file. With floppy discs the limited capacity of each one tends to compartmentalise data for you so that, provided you label the discs sensibly, it can be easily located and retrieved at a later date. With hard discs having a typical capacity of around 40 megabytes these days, finding data can be a protracted business unless the disc is sensibly organised into directories and sub-directories. In fact

you can keep branching into ever deeper levels of sub-directories indefinitely, but it is best to keep things within reason. Otherwise the use of sub-directories might make matters more difficult rather than easier. The normal way of showing the arrangement of sub-directories is to use a directory "tree", as in the example of Figure 5.1.

Chkdsk

This is a disc checking command, and it simply checks the disc in the specified drive for errors. A report on the disc is printed on the screen.

Cls

This simply clears the terminal screen, and is similar to the BASIC CLS command.

Command

This command starts the command processor (the program which contains all the internal MS-DOS commands). This instruction is usually run automatically at switch-on, and does not normally need to be run again thereafter.

Copy

Copy is one of the most frequently used commands, and it is mainly used to copy a file on one disc to another disc. It is more flexible than this though, and it can be used to copy data from any file or device to any other file or device. As a couple of examples, it is quite possible to copy input from the keyboard to a disc file, or to copy data from a disc file to a serial port.

Ctty

Normally commads are issued from the keyboard, or what is called the "console" in MS-DOS terminology. The ctty instruction enables a different source to be

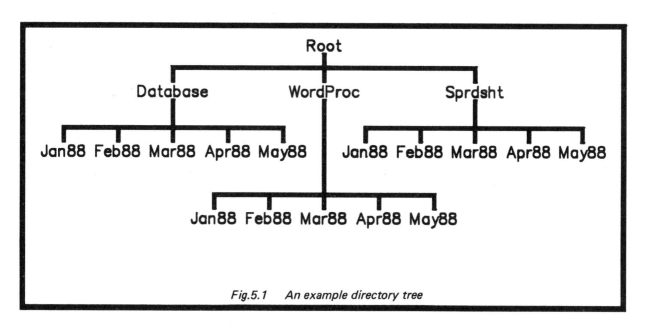

Fig.5.1   An example directory tree

61

specified as the source for commands, such as a serial port.

Date

Used to set the date on the MS-DOS clock/calendar.

Del

This is the delete command, and it deletes the specified file or group of files. Like a number of other MS-DOS commands, it accepts so-called "wildcards". This is where you use dummy characters in a filename, and MS-DOS then accepts any character in that position. The dummy character is an interrogation mark ("?"). MS-DOS filenames consist of the main name followed by an "extension", which is a further group of up to three characters. The two parts of the name are separated by a fullstop (.). Some extensions have special significance to the operating system, and must not be used out of context. There are also some conventions that it is best to adhere to. The standard MS-DOS extensions are listed below.

EXE	An executable program.
COM	An MS-DOS command (also used for any short programs).
BAT	A batch file.
SYS	A system file.
DOC	A text (document) file.
TXT	A text file.
BAK	A backup file.
BAS	A BASIC program file.
HLP	A help file.
OVL	A program overlay file.
OVR	A program overlay file.
MSG	A program message file.
$$$	A temporary file.

A "*" character can be used in place of the main file name and (or) the extension if the delete command must be applied to any main filename and (or) extension. Thus "*.*" would be used to delete all the files in a directory or on a floppy disc, and "*.BAK" would be used to delete all the backup files.

Dir

This is the directory command, and it simply lists all the files in the specified directory. It provides some basic information such as the time and date each file was created, and the amount of space left on the disc.

Diskcomp

This compares two discs and reports that they are the same, or not, as the case may be.

Diskcopy

The diskcopy command simply makes a copy of a disc. It copies the disc track by track, and sector by

sector, so that any sub-directories are copied and not just the root directory. It can only be used with floppy discs, and can not be used with hard discs.

Fdisk

The fdisk command is used to configure a hard disc for use with MS-DOS, and it must be run before a hard disc can be used with MS-DOS. Once the disc has been configured, fdisk should not be needed again.

Find

A little known but potentially useful command. It searches for a string of characters in a file or series of files (rather like the find facility found in many word processors).

Format

This command simply formats the disc in the specified drive. It is used with both floppy and hard discs.

Keybxx

In its normal state MS-DOS is configured for use with an American layout keyboard. By running the appropriate keybxx program MS-DOS can be reconfigured for a different type of keyboard (keybuk for use with U.K. layout keyboards for example).

Label

Places a volume label onto a disc. This label can be up to eleven characters in length. Like file names, letters and numbers are acceptable in labels, but these characters are not: * ? / \ ¦ . , : ; + = < > [ ] .

Mkdir

This is the make a new directory command. It does not move the system into the new directory, it simply creates it.

Mode

This sets the operating mode for certain input/output devices. It is used for such tasks as setting the baud rate and word format of serial ports, the screen display mode, and directing printer output to a serial port.

More

The more command sends output to the console (monitor screen) one screen-full at a time. The "RETURN" key is pressed to move on from one screen-full to the next.

Path

Normally MS-DOS only searches the current directory for external commands. The path command can be used to direct it to another directory if it fails to find a command program in the current directory.

Print

This command enables a file to be sent to a printer,

but it is not the same as using copy to provide this function. It provides background printing, which means that you can issue further MS-DOS commands while the operating system is working away in the background sending out data to the printer.

Prompt

The prompt command can be used to change the MS-DOS prompt. In fact it can be used to do somewhat more than this, such as changing the display colour on suitable systems.

Ren

This instruction is simply used to rename a file.

Replace

The replace command provides an easy way of replacing old files with new files. It is mainly intended for use when replacing existing software with an updated version.

Restore

As explained previously, the backup command is used to take backup copies of files. If disaster should strike and (say) the hard disc is accidentally formatted (which removes its previous contents), restore is the command that is used to take the data on the backup discs and replace it on the hard disc.

Rmdir

This is rather like the delete command, but it is for directories and not files. You can not remove a directory unless all the files in it have been deleted (a factor which is common to all the operating systems I have encountered).

Sort

Using this command the contents of a file are read, sorted into alphabetical order, and then printed out on the screen of the monitor.

Tree

The tree command lists the path of each directory and sub-directory on the specified drive. It just gives a list, it does not draw out a directory tree diagram!

Type

This command displays the contents of a file on the screen. With a large file the screen will probably scroll far too rapidly to permit its contents to be read properly. Pressing "CONTROL" and "s" can be used to start and stop the "typing", as required (or the "more" command can be issued together with the "type" command).

Ver

Issuing the ver (version) command simply results in the particular version of MS-DOS in use being printed on the screen.

Verify

This command turns the verify switch on or off. In other words, when data is written to a disc the computer verifies that the data has been successfully stored on disc, and gives a warning message if it can not be stored on disc in uncorrupted form.

Vol

This command merely displays the volume label of a disc, if it has one.

Xcopy

The xcopy command is much the same as the copy command. They differ in that xcopy, unless instructed otherwise, copies all files in the specified directory, and will also copy any sub-directories.

Batch Files

This should give you a good idea of the kind of tasks that can be handled via the operating system, but this is only a rather superficial look at what is quite a complex subject. Most operating systems have a lot of subtle and potentially very useful features. A very useful feature of MS-DOS is its batch files. This is where a series of instructions are contained in a disc file having "BAT" as its extension. By typing the name of the file it is run by the computer which then follows the list of instructions just as if they were typed from the keyboard. If a batch file called "AUTOEXEC.BAT" is placed in the root directory, this will be run automatically at switch-on, as soon as the MS-DOS command processor has been loaded. This is useful for automatically loading any software that must always be run at switch-on. This includes memory resident programs, mouse drivers, etc. If a computer is only used with one applications program, this facility can be used to automatically load and run this program at switch-on.

WIMPs

Although operating systems provide a wide range of very valuable features, they tend to be difficult to learn and use. Some quite simple tasks can require a long and complicated command to be typed into the computer. In an attempt to make their computers easier to use, some manufacturers now supply them with WIMP based "user interfaces". These are also available as add-ons for some computers that do not have them as standard. GEM of the Amstrad PCs and the Atari ST range is an example of a WIMP based user interface, as is the Amiga's "Workbench".

WIMP stands for "Windows – Icons – Mouse – Pointer". A window is merely an area of screen which is given over to a particular function, and an icon is a graphical representation of something. For example, a disc would be represented by a simple graphical representation of a floppy disc. This type of user interface differs from a conventional operating system in that it uses a graphics screen rather than a text screen. Wherever possible icons tend to be

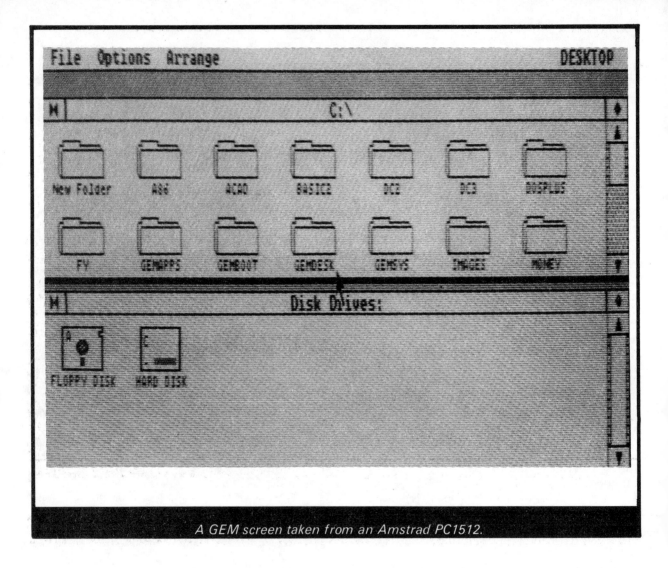

A GEM screen taken from an Amstrad PC1512.

used instead of text, but text can (and often is) mixed in with the graphics where it is helpful in clarifying matters. The mouse, as no doubt most computer users are aware, is a small box which is moved around on the desk top in order to move the on-screen pointer to the desired position. The pointer is sometimes a simple arrow shape, or it can be something a little more elaborate. Either way its function is just the same – it indicates which icon you wish to manipulate. The mouse has two or three control buttons which are used to indicate when the pointer is over the desired icon, and things of this nature.

With a WIMP based operating system you would normally run a program by placing the program disc in (say) drive A, and then double "clicking" on the drive A icon. Double "clicking" simply means placing the pointer over an icon and then pressing the left mouse button twice in rapid succession. Doing this on the drive A icon does not run the program, it opens a window in which the contents of the disc are displayed in icon form. Some of the icons might be

for "drawers" or "folders", which are sub-directories in normal computer terminology. Double "clicking" on one of these opens another window and displays its contents. This might reveal icons for further sub-directories, which can then be opened by double "clicking" them. To run a program you must double "click" on its icon.

Copying a file from one disc to another is quite straightforward. First windows for the two discs must be opened, and if the file to be copied is in a directory or sub-directory, a window for that directory must be opened. Similarly, if you wish to copy the file into a sub-directory, then a window for that sub-directory must be opened on the destination disc. To copy a file you drag its icon to the window for the disc and (where appropriate) directory or sub-directory you wish to copy it to. Dragging merely means positioning the pointer over the icon, pressing the left mouse button, and then moving the mouse/pointer. The icon will move with the pointer. Deleting a file is usually similar, with the icon for the unwanted file being dragged to a "trashcan" icon.

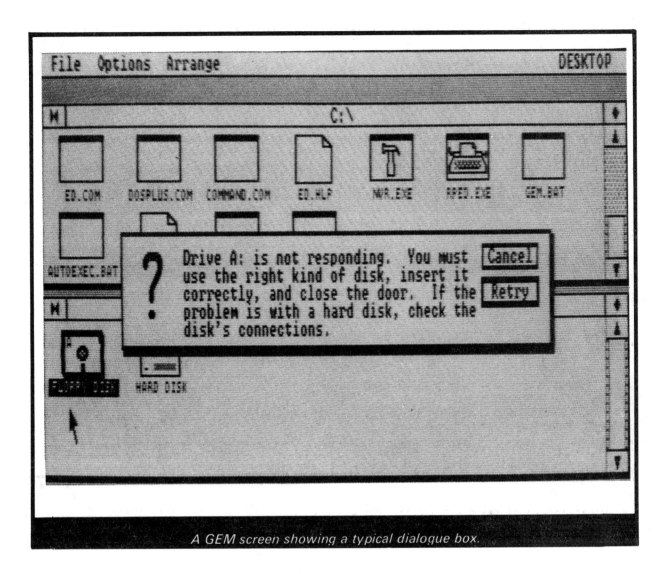

C:\

ED.COM   DOSPLUS.COM   COMMAND.COM   ED.HLP   NVR.EXE   RPED.EXE   GEM.BAT

AUTOEXEC.BAT

? Drive A: is not responding. You must
use the right kind of disk, insert it
correctly, and close the door. If the
problem is with a hard disk, check the
disk's connections.

[Cancel]

[Retry]

FLOPPY DISK   HARD DISK

A GEM screen showing a typical dialogue box.

To increase the features available from a WIMP based operating system it is usually backed-up with a pop-down menu system which permits facilities such as disk renaming and formatting to be accomplished. A good WIMP based operating system is very versatile, but is probably somewhat less so than a text based system. Some computers offer both environments as standard. The Commodore Amiga computers for example, have their "Workbench" WIMP user interface for beginners, and a command line interpreter (CLI) for experienced users.

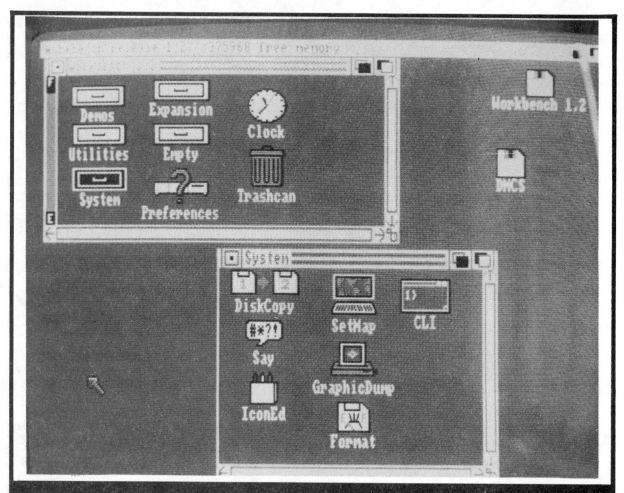

The Amiga's Workbench user interface. The system "drawer" in the upper "window" has been "opened". The lower "window" shows its contents.

Desk File **View** Options

✓ Show as Icons
Show as Text

✓ Sort by Name
Sort by Date
Sort by Size
Sort by Type

A:\

174 ... n 20 items.

FLOPPY DISK

FLOPPY DISK

FASTERS.PRG GEMDEMO.RSC HARMON.RSC HARMON1.RSC

MIDIDELE.SC MIDIFILT.RSC MIDIREAD.RSC MIDISTEP.RSC MIDITERM.RSC OUTCHAN.RSC

PRGCHNG2.RSC PROG1.RSC SPLIT.RSC SPLIT2.RSC SPLIT3.RSC VELOCITY.RSC

B:\

459555 bytes used in 9 items.

CR3.RSC CREATOR.RSC CREAT_02.RSC DEMO7.SON NOTATOR.FNT NOTATOR.PRG

SUP16.RSC

TRASH

*GEM on the Atari ST in the high resolution screen mode.
Note the pop-down menu at the top of the screen.*

67

Chapter 6

COMPUTER GRAPHICS

Block Graphics

In the beginning there were flashing lights on panels, then the teletype, then line printers, but with the arrival of the Visual Display Unit (VDU) with cathode ray tube came the possibility of computers displaying graphics as well as text. The first graphics on home computers, however, were based on text displays and took the form of modified characters. These characters were in the form of blocks of various types, and were intended to be used to form decorative lines on displays. They were printed on the screen just like the normal alphanumeric characters. By using suitable combinations, single and multiple lines, broken lines and checkered patterns could be produced.

A further development of this was to allow users to design their own character patterns. The block shapes were stored in memory as bit patterns, and could be modified by poking new values into the appropriate memory locations. Often this could be quite involved, as the bit patterns started off in ROM. To modify them, the entire character set had to be copied into RAM, some or all of the characters altered, and the computer then instructed to use the new set in RAM.

An advantage of block graphics is that it does not require a lot of memory to store the video display. Each character needs only one byte of memory, so a 40 x 25 character display needs less than 1k of memory. A byte can hold values from 0 to 255, so 256 possible characters could be displayed, though character sets would normally be smaller than this. It is normal for the first 128 characters to be the normal alphanumeric characters, punctuation marks,

The block graphics on the Sinclair ZX81 can be entered direct from the keyboard, and are seen here marked on the keys.

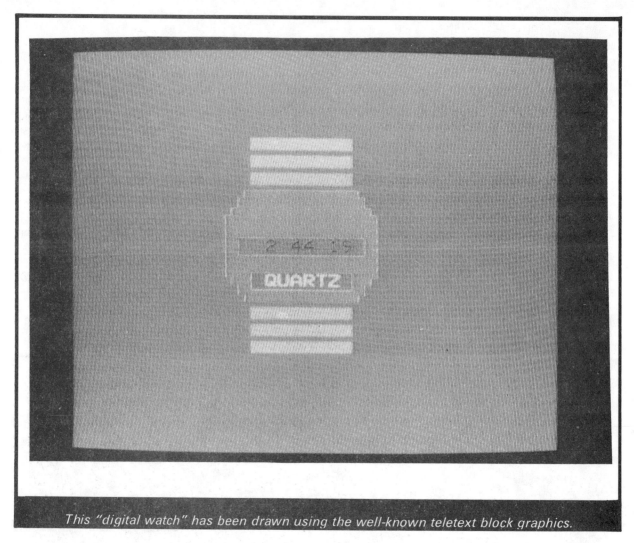

This "digital watch" has been drawn using the well-known teletext block graphics.

etc. and for the second 128 to contain the graphics characters (however values below 32 are not normally used for printable characters).

Many early animated computer games were written using user-defined characters. Such animation was not particularly smooth, as the characters could only be moved by a smallest increment of one character space, across or up/down, but fast action was possible, even with programs written in BASIC. A feature of block graphics is that the circuitry which generates the display has to refer to the character definition table in memory each time a frame is sent to the VDU, which is usually 25 times a second. If the character tables are altered, the characters on screen will alter. This was frequently used in games to make the aliens, monsters or whatever wave their arms as they attacked.

Block graphics have not entirely died out. There are graphics characters in the character set of the IBM PC, and printers intended for use with this computer can even print out these characters (this includes some daisy wheel types). However, perhaps the best-known example of block graphics remaining

are the teletext graphics, familiar from the Oracle and CEEFAX TV displays. The BBC microcomputers also have these characters built in, and these teletext or mode 7 graphics have something of a cult following among some BBC users.

A special feature of teletext graphics is the use of 'serial attributes'. Some characters in the set do not appear as characters (their places in the display appear as spaces in background colour), but they alter the appearance of whatever comes after them on the same display line. They can alter foreground and background colours, set flashing on or off, and change the display to double-height characters (this requires printing exactly the same thing on two consecutive lines). These serial attributes allow a sophisticated 8-colour display to be built up, while still requiring just 1000 bytes to store a 40 x 25 screen.

Block graphics, however, really belong to the days when memory was expensive, and 16K was a lot of RAM. Now that large memories are the norm, more sophisticated graphics are provided.

Bit-Mapped Graphics

When a reasonable amount of memory can be set aside for the graphics display, it is possible to use a system where each point which can be displayed on the screen is controlled by one bit in memory. If the bit is set, the point will appear as foreground, if it is clear it will appear as background. This is the basis of a bit-mapped display. On this type of display, as well as displaying the normal text characters, it is possible to draw lines, and also to fill large areas, that is, display them in foreground colour.

In theory it is perfectly straightforward to display text characters on a graphics screen, and in practice most computers with bit-mapped displays offer this facility. It is often possible to place text anywhere on the screen, not just on the standard text lines and columns. This is useful for labelling graphs and similar uses, and, in conjunction with user-defined characters, for smooth pixel-by-pixel animations. User-defined characters can still be used to produce aliens and monsters, but changing the character definition in memory will not change the appearance of characters already on the screen, so making them wave their arms needs extra programming!

It is common for computers which offer high-resolution bit mapped displays also to have text-only display modes, which normally use much less memory and are useful for applications like word-processing where graphics are not required and the memory freed can be used to store larger documents.

There were a few early computers which had separate text and graphics modes, and which did not allow text easily to be displayed in the graphics mode. Notable among these was the Dragon. The standard way of getting around this was to draw text onto the screen using the line drawing commands. This was effective, but a bit of a nuisance, and probably played a part in the demise of this machine.

Bit-mapped displays do need a fair amount of memory. A display capable of showing 640 points horizontally by 200 vertically (this is a common type of display) needs 128000 bits, which is 16K. (In fact, it is 16000 bytes whereas 16K is actually 16 x 1024 or 16384 bytes, but it would be normal to reserve a

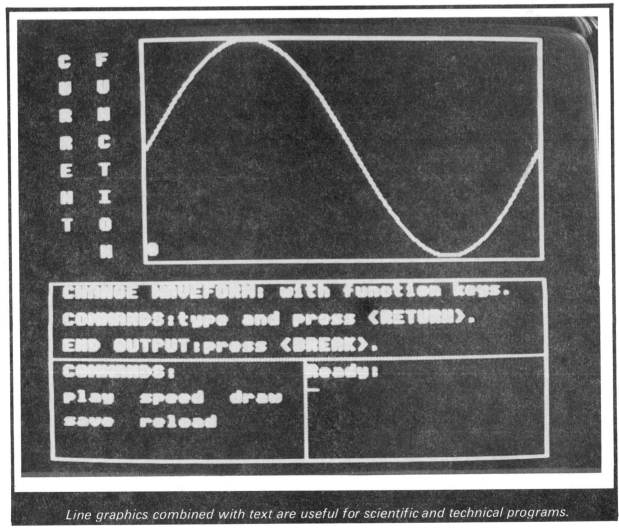

Line graphics combined with text are useful for scientific and technical programs.

An example of user-defined characters, in conjunction with line/fill graphics, to produce a game display.

full 16K block for this size of display.)

A true bit-mapped display of this type is only capable of showing two colours, foreground and background. If a colour display is required, more bits are needed for each point. It is common to find computers offering several display modes. Either more memory is required for more colours at the same resolution, or a fixed amount of memory is used for the display, and there is a trade-off between the number of colours which can be displayed and the available resolution. This second system is the more common. One popular range of computers offers three modes, either 640 x 200 in two colours (1 bit per point), 320 x 200 in four colours (2 bits per point), or 160 x 200 in 16 colours (4 bits per point). Such displays are still, however, called bit-mapped.

Though such a display is limited to two, four or 16 colours at any one time, it is usually possible to choose the colours to be displayed from a "palette" which contains many more colours. The values stored in screen memory are called the logical colour numbers, and the numbers of the colours in the palette are called the actual or physical colours. The colours for the display are selected by assigning actual colours to physical colours.

This is often likened to having a limited number of pens, each of which can be filled from a larger number of bottles of ink. The number of colours you can draw in at any one time is limited by the number of pens, but you can empty a pen and fill it with a different ink. This is not a very good analogy, however, as if you change the colour of ink in a pen (assign a different actual colour to a logical colour) anything drawn on the screen in the original ink will change to the new colour. This last fact can be put to good use, however, especially in games. For instance, by changing an assigned colour from a foreground colour to the background colour, things can be made to appear and disappear instantly.

Extended Colour Systems

If a large number of colours are required in a display, as is often needed in games, the choice of needing either to use a large area of memory or limit the resolution becomes a problem. If the area of memory becomes very large, firstly not much room is left for anything else, and secondly, the large manipulations needed for animation will tend to make game play sluggish. For these reasons, several methods have been devised to allow more colours to appear on screen with less memory overhead.

In a system where a small number of colours selected from a larger palette can be displayed, the actual assignment is done by part of the computer hardware as the screen image is sent to the VDU. A simple way of showing more colours is to cause this hardware device to use a different selection of colours for different parts of the picture. This is done by timing, often by use of interrupts. Because of the way in which the picture is built up on the VDU screen, in horizontal lines from top to bottom, the colours usually can only be altered in horizontal bands across the screen.

An extension of this system is to allow each screen line to have its own set of assigned colours. This does require some extra memory, as the colour assignments for each line must be stored, but the overhead is small, and displays using this system can be very impressive. With both these methods some care is, however, necessary, as object blocks moving down the screen could easily change colour as they move through areas with different assignments.

An alternative system is the use of "parallel attributes". This system is used by the Sinclair Spectrum, and is based on the text screen display. Each character position has a set of attributes which control the foreground and background colour for that position, and also the degree of intensity (normal or bright) and whether steady or flashing. Thus you can have only two colours in each position, but all the available colours can be displayed simultaneously. The attributes for each position are set automatically as a line is drawn through that position (or a character printed), and this causes one limitation of the system. If you have drawn through a position in one colour, and subsequently drawn through it in another colour, the part of the original line passing through that

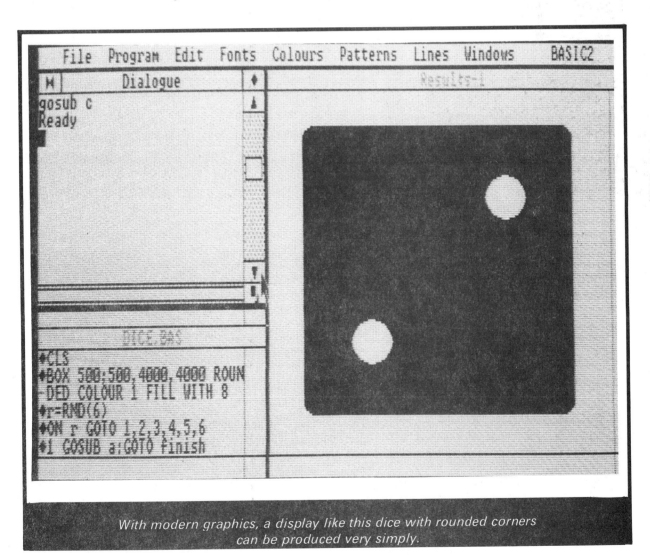

With modern graphics, a display like this dice with rounded corners can be produced very simply.

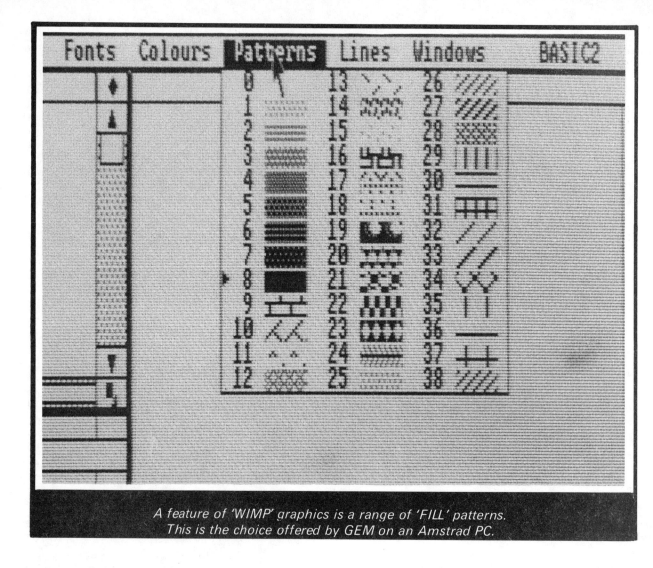

A feature of 'WIMP' graphics is a range of 'FILL' patterns.
This is the choice offered by GEM on an Amstrad PC.

position will change to the new colour.

The serial attribute system of the teletext display system has been used just once in a high-resolution graphics display, on the Oric and Atmos series of computers (which used the teletext system for their text display). Each serial attribute was only one pixel deep, but eight pixels wide, aligned on character position boundaries. As the positions occupied by the attributes appeared in background colour only this placed a lot of limitations on screen displays, and could not be considered a great success.

Sprites

Sprites, also called Moveable Object Blocks or MOBs, belong to the golden age of animated games, now past. In some ways a sprite is similar to a user-defined character in that it has a shape defined as a bit pattern in memory, but in most cases it can be larger than a character, and it may also be able to be multi-coloured. The way in which sprites are implemented can differ from machine to machine, but in general they do not form part of the bit-mapped screen memory. They are added to the display by a hardware device.

Sprites can be moved around the screen display smoothly, and it is not necessary to erase them from a previous position before moving them to a new one, which makes programming very easy. In fact, in the most sophisticated implementation, the sprite can be given a velocity and direction, and the hardware takes care of all movement. The hardware device also signals to the program, either by a form of interrupt or by use of flags, when two sprites collide or when a sprite passes over a particular colour on the main display. This makes it possible to detect when a 'hit' has occurred.

It is interesting that although in the great home computer boom of the early eighties many machines with sprite systems were available, none was ever supplied with a version of BASIC which allowed all the sprite facilities to be exploited.

Windows

Windowing is a method of allowing the total screen

areas to be divided up into two or more smaller areas which can be separately controlled. In particular it allows part of the screen to be designed as a text window and part as a graphics window. Text can then be printed in the text window without having to specify exactly where on the screen it will be printed, and the text screen allowed to fill up and scroll, without any risk of the graphics window being corrupted by text being printed across the display. It should, however, be mentioned that with most simple windowing systems the windows can overlap, and it is up to the programmer to ensure that they do not unless intended.

Where windowing is based on a bit-mapped screen display, the windows will normally have to display the same colours, unless one of the extended colour methods described above is in operation.

A more sophisticated form of windowing is now common. In simple windowing, if text scrolls out of a text window it is lost, and if anything is written over the contents of a graphics window the graphics is lost. In the more sophisticated systems, the printed text which scrolls out of the window is stored, and it is possible to scroll up and down through the contents, usually by use of a mouse, but cursor key control is also provided. It is also possible with these systems to open one window on top of another window, and subsequently close it, and to have the contents of the first window restored.

A further feature of these systems is that window sizes and positions can be controlled by the user, usually again by means of a mouse. If a window is made smaller, all the original contents is stored, and if the window is subsequently restored to its original size, all the original contents will be redrawn, both text and graphics.

These advanced windowing systems are normally provided as part of operating system front ends. In addition to the windowing, simplified file-handling facilities are normally provided, together with advanced graphics facilities such as text fonts in a variety of styles and sizes, line styles for drawing (solid in various widths, dotted, dashed), and patterns for area fills. The first such system to gain popularity was the operating system for the Apple Macintosh, and this has been followed by DR GEM and Microsoft WINDOWS, among others.

Co-Ordinate Systems

In any graphics system, some means is needed to specify where on the screen drawing is to be done. Positions on the screen are specified by systems of co-ordinates. On a graphics screen, drawing is done at the position of the cursor. Unlike the cursors on text screens, which are normally visible, graphics cursors are normally purely notional and not displayed, though some of the recent windowing systems do display a crosshair cursor unless instructed otherwise. In drawing a line or moving to a new position on the screen, the co-ordinates specify how far the cursor is

to move, either relative to its current position or relative to a graphics origin, the point which has co-ordinates of 0, 0.

When the new position of the cursor is specified in terms of how far it is to move from its current position, this is termed relative co-ordinates. This system is generally more difficult to work with than the alternative system of specifying the position relative to a graphics origin. It is found mostly on lower-priced computers like the Sinclair Spectrum. When drawing on the screen, it is usually necessary to use two variables to keep track of the absolute position of the cursor on the screen, as computers with relative co-ordinate systems also tend to be the ones which generate an error if you try to draw to a position off the screen.

When new positions for the graphics cursor are specified relative to a graphics origin, this is termed absolute co-ordinates. This system is generally quite easy to use. The position of the graphics origin is normally the extreme bottom left-hand corner of the screen, in contradistinction to the usual text co-ordinate system which has its origin in the top left-hand corner. Some computers allow the user to specify the position of the graphics origin on the screen. If the origin is in the conventional position, only positive co-ordinates are required. If it is moved anywhere else, both positive and negative co-ordinates are needed in order to be able to specify any point on the screen. For some purposes, it is convenient to move the graphics origin to the centre of the screen.

Whether relative or absolute co-ordinates are being used, it is conventional to give the horizontal co-ordinate first, followed by the vertical co-ordinate. These are conventionally termed the X direction or axis (X is a cross) and the Y direction or axis (Y's up).

A further system which should be mentioned is the system of turtle graphics which has its origin in the LOGO computer language. This is not really a co-ordinate system, but is one in which the cursor, which is called a 'turtle', is moved around the screen by commands which indicate how far it should move, forward or backward, and angles through which it should turn, right or left, normally specified in degrees. This type of graphics is now included in some other languages, in particular in some recent versions of BASIC. (In fact, some versions of LOGO also allow the turtle to be placed using a system of absolute co-ordinates.) This type of graphics was designed as a learning aid, and apart from this is limited in application.

It may seem obvious to match the co-ordinate system to the resolution of the screen image, so that a change of 1 unit equtes to a movement of 1 pixel, and simple computers with one screen mode frequently do use a system of this sort. Where there are several screen modes with different resolutions, however, if graphics originally written for one mode were displayed in another mode, the size would alter, and in many cases the shape too, as changes in screen resolution with mode in many cases only affect resolution in one direction. In such cases, the co-ordinate system used may have more points than can be resolved by the display in any mode, and the number of points per pixel will change with mode, but the size and shape of the graphics will remain constant.

This also allows another problem to be solved, the fact that pixels are frequently not square. If a co-ordinate system based on pixels is used, and the pixels on the screen are in fact wider than they are high, if you drew a circle using the usual formulae, it would appear as an ellipse. If the co-ordinate system is non-pixel based, it can be adjusted so that equal changes in co-ordinates do equate to equal distances on the screen in both horizontal and vertical directions, and circles will then be circles.

A good example of this is the **BBC** microcomputer. This has graphics modes with resolutions of 640 x 256, 320 x 256 and 160 x 256. It uses a co-ordinate system with 1280 points by 1024, and these do relate to equal distances on the screen. In the highest resolution mode the pixels are 2 units wide by 4 high, in the middle mode they are 4 units wide by 4 high — a rare case of truly square pixels — and in the lowest resolution they are 8 units wide by 4 high.

In some of the latest versions of **BASIC** for use with windowing environments much smaller points are used for specifying positions. In **BASIC 2** on the Amstrad PCs, which runs under **GEM**, a co-ordinate system with 5000 units along the shorter dimension of a window, and as many as necessary along the longer dimension to ensure equal increments, is used. These high values are used in part because these environments are designed to allow output to be sent to devices other than the screen with little or no re-writing. Some other devices, such as laser printers and pen plotters, can have a resolution very much higher than a **VDU** screen. Using these very fine co-ordinates allows these devices to be used to their full potential.

Chapter 7

LEXICON

Absolute Addressing

In assembly language and machine code programming, absolute addressing is the address mode in which the address of the data is given directly in the instruction. It is sometimes also called direct addressing.

Acoustic Coupler

This is a form of modem, but it refers specifically to a type which is not connected directly to the telephone system. Instead it has a receptacle for a telephone handset. Signals from the computer (usually sent and received via an RS232C serial port) are converted into tones which are fed to the mouthpiece, while the tones from the earpiece are decoded and fed to the computer.

With all other factors being equal, this generally works a little less reliably than a modem that connects directly to the telephone lines. On the other hand, it gives convenience, and can be used anywhere where a telephone having a reasonably standard handset is available. I suppose that strictly speaking the acoustic coupler is only the part that actually couples the audio tones into the handset, and picks up the tones from the earpiece. However, this term seems to be applied to a complete modem which uses this method of coupling.

ANDing

See "BITWISE".

Artificial Intelligence

A branch of programming which deals with programs which "learn" or which can seem to "think" about a problem and make an intelligent decision. The most common applications of artificial intelligence are the "expert system" type of database. This is an area in which there is much controversy. On the one hand, some people think that it is wrong to consider a machine to have any kind of intelligence, and prefer the term "applied intelligence". On the other hand, some artificial intelligence lobbyists have suggested that computers running this type of software have a form of sentience and should be considered a new life-form.

ARM

This is an acronym standing for Acorn Reduced instruction set Machine, and it is the RISC type microprocessor used in the Acorn Archimedes series of computers. These machines stand as excellent justification of the claims for speed made for RISC chips.

Array

The term "array" is mostly used in BASIC programming, but it is also used elsewhere. It refers to a form of variable by which tabular data may be easily stored and manipulated. An array consists of a number of variables of one type, which have a common name and are distinguished from each other by numbers called subscripts. These subscripts represent the positions of the individual variables, called elements, in the table. Arrays can have one or more dimensions, with each element having a subscript for each dimension. A single dimension array would have only one subscript, and would be analogous to a simple list. A two-dimensional array is analogous to a table with rows down the page and columns across it. Each element would have two subscripts, giving its row number and column number. A three dimensional array can be thought of as like a number of pages of rows and columns, and a four dimensional array as a number of books, each with a number of pages. Different versions of BASIC differ in the number of dimensions allowable and the number of elements allowed in each dimension. The number of elements allowed is often limited to 255, but may be higher on 16-bit computers. The number of dimensions allowed may be limited to one or two, or to 255, or limited only by the available memory. In most versions of BASIC, the subscripts are given in brackets after the variable name used to identify the array, the individual subscripts being separated by commas. Generally, both string and numeric arrays are possible, but all elements must be of one type. In some BASICs, elements of string arrays must be of fixed length, and in other (primitive) versions, string arrays are not supported.

ASCII

These letters stand for "American Standard Code for Information Interchange". Computers do not store and manipulate text as such, but deal with all information in the form of binary numbers. Text is handled using a simple code whereby each text character (including such things as line feeds and carriage returns) is assigned an individual code number. For example, the ASCII code for "U" is 01010101 in binary, which is equivalent to 85 in the ordinary decimal numbering system. If you should ever need to deal with ASCII codes, it will almost certainly be with them in their decimal form rather than as raw binary numbers. The ASCII codes are now almost universally accepted as the standard set of text code numbers, but information in ASCII form is not necessarily fully compatible between one system and another. Many word processors and other text handling programs use additional codes when formatting the text instead of using large numbers of line feeds, carriage returns, and spaces. This gives more compact text files, but it does mean that the control codes of one program may not be understood by another program. This may simply result in oddly formatted text (with perhaps a few odd looking characters mixed in with the text), or in an extreme case it could cause the program to hang up. Some text processing programs have a facility for storing and retrieving text in pure ASCII form. Some also have conversion facilities so that they can produce files that are compatible with popular text processing programs.

Assembler

Many programs are written in a high level computer language (such as BASIC) which makes the job of programming very much easier. The alternative is to program in machine language (also known as machine code). This means directly programming the microprocessor at the heart of the computer with its instruction code numbers. Machine code is not really practical for anything other than very short routines, and it is usual for assembly language to be used. This is essentially the same as machine code, but a program called an "assembler" is used to convert easily remembered mnemonics into the corresponding machine code numbers. In fact most assemblers provide a bit more help than this, but assembly language programming is something that is restricted to those who are prepared to learn about computers in some detail. The advertising for some programs boast that they are largely written in assembly language, and the advantages of assembly language are more for the user than the programmer. There is really only one advantage, and this is speed. The computer is simply executing the program, without having to do any interpreting from a high level computer language into machine code instructions as it goes along. Assembly language programs are therefore very fast — as fast as the computer can run in fact.

Auto-Dial

This is a feature of many modems. As this term implies, the modem automatically dials the required number. In fact these days it is more usually the computer that controls things, and the store of numbers are held in the computer. In this case, both the software and the modem must support auto-dialling if it is to function properly.

Axis

This is the term used in computer graphics to refer to the direction in which specified co-ordinates apply. The X-axis runs horizontally across the screen, and the Y-axis runs vertically down it. Note that the axis has direction, but not position. The axis is *not* a line running half-way up or half-way across the screen. Conventionally, in giving the co-ordinates of a point,

the X-axis co-ordinate is given first, followed by the Y-co-ordinate. In three-dimensional graphics, the third axis, the direction perpendicular to the screen surface, is called the Z-axis. Of course, it is not really possible to draw in 3-D on a flat screen, but forms of perspective drawing can be programmed.

Background (Printing)

Some programs have the ability to send data to the printer and at the same time get on with other jobs. With a word-processor, for example, you may be able to print one document while writing or editing another. This is called background printing. You may be able to specify a list of files to be printed, one after another, while getting on with other things. Some operating systems may allow a general facility to do this with all programs, and it may be possible to print graphics files as well as text. This can be a great time-saver, but it may be found that program execution may be slowed while printing is in progress, or that printing slows or temporarily stops when a program is active (i.e. not waiting for you to press a key). This is especially true with graphics output. (See also SPOOLER)

Background (Program)

A background program is one which is resident in memory and is running all the time, but generally does not produce any output, so that the user is not aware of it, but can be called upon when necessary. The most obvious example is a real-time clock. There are also background alarm programs which can be set to alert the user at some given time, provided, of course, that the computer is in use at that time. (See also RESIDENT, MULTI-TASKING)

Back-Up

As a noun, this is a copy of software or data which is kept as insurance in case something happens to the original. Data and programs are normally backed-up on floppy discs, but for hard disc users there are tape streamers which will back-up the entire disc much more rapidly and with far less effort on the part of the operator. As a verb, this term means the actual act of making back-up discs (or whatever). A less than interesting task, but one that should be done fastidiously. It is easy to overlook just how much data a floppy disc can hold until one becomes damaged. Losing the entire contents of a hard disc with no back-up data available does not bear thinking about.

BASIC

A popular programming language for beginners. BASIC stands for "beginners all-purpose symbolic instruction code". This is the most generally accepted explanation of the name, but is not universally accepted. Although it has received a fair amount of criticism over recent years, good BASIC languages are relatively easy to learn and are very versatile. A lot of the criticisms aimed at BASIC are really only valid when applied to early implementations of the language which are now mostly obsolete. BASIC programs tend to be quite slow in operation, although a modern interpreted BASIC running on one of today's more powerful microcomputers can run fast enough for many requirements. BASIC compilers are available for many computers these days, and these provide a very respectable operating speed. Maybe it is not the ideal computing language for professional programmers, but its success with home computer users speaks for itself.

Baud Rate
This is a term that applies to serial communications ports, such as the RS232C and similar RS423 serial ports that are fitted to many computers. It is a measure of the speed at which data is sent from a port, and it is merely the number of bits sent per second (assuming a continuous data stream). Many modems, for example, work with a baud rate of 1200, or 1200 bits per second. Note that seven or eight bits are required for a complete byte of data (e.g. an ASCII character), and timing bits accompany each byte. Thus about ten bits are required per character, and 1200 baud only represents about 120 characters per second, not 1200. RS232C serial ports are asynchronous types. To the user the practical importance of this is that the system relies on the baud rate at which data is being transmitted accurately matching that to which the receiving equipment is set. For this system to be workable it is essential to have standardised baud rates, and there is a wide range of these running from 50 to 19200 baud. Although it might seem better to have just one standard baud rate, serial links are used with a wide variety of equipment types. A standard rate that might be painfully slow for one piece of equipment could be impractically high for another. The standard baud rates are 50, 75, 110, 150, 300, 600, 1200, 1800, 2400, 4800, 9600, and 19200 baud. Most of these are available from the majority of computer serial ports, but one or two are usually unobtainable (the highest and slowest rates are often absent). Peripherals such as printers and plotters which have a serial interface often only provide a very limited range of baud rates. It is then a matter of setting up the computer to suit the peripheral device.

Binary
Computers handle data in what is really a rather crude form, with electronics circuits that provide a low output voltage (about 0.8 volts or less) to represent 0, or a higher voltage (about 3 to 5 volts) to represent 1. This is very convenient from the point of view of designing the electronics, but the normal decimal system can not be accommodated by a system which only allows each digit to be 0 or 1. Instead the binary system of numbering has to be used. Whereas the columns of figures in the decimal system represent the number of units, tens, hundreds, thousands, etc., in the binary system they represent the number of units, twos, fours, eights, sixteens, and so on. This enables any desired number to be represented, but it requires a large number of digits when compared to the decimal system. This is the only practical way of handling things with the present technology though. Each binary digit is usually given its abbreviated name of a "bit". Data is often manipulated in the form of 8 bit numbers, or "bytes" as these are generally termed. With 8 bits, numbers in the range 0 to 255 can be catered for, and with 16 bits, numbers from 0 to 65535 can be accommodated. In fact numbers of any magnitude can be handled by an 8 or 16 bits computer, but only by using several bytes to represent large numbers, and processing the data one byte (or 16 bit "word") at a time. Unless you get involved in programming this is all of academic importance, and is not something that is normally encountered when running applications software. The hardware converts data input in decimal form into binary, and converts any binary numbers into decimal before they are output. The fact that the computer is operating using binary data is therefore not apparent to the user.

Bit
A contraction of BInary digiT. See BINARY above.

Bitwise
This is where two binary numbers are compared on a bit by bit basis, and the answer depends on the logic states of each pair of bits. With bitwise ANDing, a 1 is placed in the answer only if both bits are at logic 1. Bitwise ORing is similar, but a 1 is placed in the answer if either or both bits that are compared are at logic 1. XORing is almost the same as ORing, but a 1 is placed in the answer only if a 1 is present in one or other of the ORed numbers. Unlike bitwise ORing, with XORing a 0 is placed in the answer if both the compared bits are at logic 1. Bitwise ANDing is used where only one bit (or perhaps a few bits) of a byte must be read. All three types of bitwise manipulation can be used in graphics programs to obtain various effects.

Blitter
The term "blitter" derives from "bit image manipulator". It is a hardware device which is used for moving blocks of memory around rapidly, without requiring action from the computer CPU. Blitters can also provide bitwise ANDing, ORing etc. on areas of memory. It is mostly used for rapid movement of parts of the VDU screen image, giving effects similar to, but more sophisticated than, sprite animation. It is therefore mainly regarded as a graphics device, but could also be used for other things.

Boot

This is a slightly vague term, but one which is generally accepted as being the process by which an operating system seems to load itself from disc and into the computer at switch-on. This is likened to someone lifting themselves up by their bootstraps, and is sometimes given the alternative name of "bootstrapping". Of course, the disc operating system does not really load itself at switch-on, and there is a very basic operating system in the computer which loads the disc system. The disc operating system then takes over control from the built-in start-up routine.

Brush

Brush in a computer context is a paint program term. Although mainly associated with the Amiga computer, it now seems to be gaining a wider acceptance. As the name suggests, it is the notional object with which the drawing is painted. However, some paint programs enable quite complex "brushes" to be used. Not only can quite complex shapes be used, multiple colours can be used within the shape. In some cases you can select an area of a drawing and then use that as a brush.

Buffer

This is another term which is a little imprecise in its meaning, but it is most often used to refer to a block of memory. This memory does not have to be in the computer, and many printers incorporate a buffer. With these the idea is that the computer can rapidly load a document into the printer's buffer, and the printer can then print it out while the computer is then free to get on with other tasks. There are also buffers within computers, such as the keyboard buffer. Characters typed into the keyboard are often stored in a buffer and read from this, rather than being read direct from the keyboard and acted upon immediately. This reduces the risk of characters being missed when demands on the computer are high. Even so, if you type data into the computer at the wrong time it may well be overlooked and not acted upon.

Bug

A general term for a fault in a computer system, but one which is generally applied to problems with software.

Bulletin Board

This is a system that can be accessed by anyone who has a suitable computer and modem simply by dialing up the appropriate number. There are a fair number of these at present, mostly run by computer enthusiasts. A few are run by companies or technology departments of schools, colleges, and universities. The facilities offered vary enormously from one to another. The "bulletin board" name is derived from the basic facility of being able to leave messages which can be read by anyone who accesses the system. If you are having difficulty with your computer system for example, you could leave details of the problem with a request (plea?) for help from anyone who has experienced the same problem and found a solution. Some services offer free software which can be down-loaded into your computer. The type of service that is most likely to be of real benefit to you is one which specialises in software and general information for your particular type of computer, or one which serves some other specialist interest of yours.

Byte

Eight binary digits (bits). See BINARY.

C

A compiled programming language. Most implementations of C are very fast, and a lot of commercial software is written in this language. It is not really a beginner's language, but most people who have some programming experience with BASIC and assembler find it reasonably easy to master. It is a very versatile language, but is considered to be rather too low level by some programmers. It is very "portable".

CAD

Either "computer aided drawing", "computer aided drafting", or "computer aided design". The first two are really the same, and mean a sort of computer equivalent of an ordinary drawing board, paper, and pen. A CAD system is more versatile than conventional methods of drawing in that it is much easier to make changes to a drawing. It is really the drawing equivalent of a word processor. CAD seems to have become very popular in recent times, and modern CAD programs and output devices can provide some very good results. Even low cost systems are quite capable these days. The drawings in this book were produced using a CAD system incidentally.

Computer aided design generally means mathematically modelling something to check that it works before it is made. Making and testing some types of equipment is so expensive that this is the only practical way of doing things. As yet it is only something that is used in a few specialist areas of interest, and many CAD systems of this type are custom built one-offs!

Camera Device

A camera device is a peripheral device which is usually connected to the monitor output of a computer, and is used to produce photographic slides or prints of screen output onto (usually) 35mm photographic film. The camera device contains its own picture tube and lens system. The film transport may also be built-in or it may be in the form of a conventional camera body (usually of single lens reflex type) which attaches to the device. The main benefit of using a camera device is the avoidance of the distortion which normally occurs if a monitor screen is simply photographed with a camera, and also the banding which can result from a mismatch between the shutter speed used and the scan rate of the monitor. The definition will be the same as the screen definition. Camera devices can be very expensive, and are only worthwhile where large numbers of screen pictures are required on a regular basis.

Centronics
This is a form of interface, and it is sometimes called a "parallel" interface. The Centronics name is that of a printer manufacturer who pioneered this type of interface, but it is now the accepted standard for printers, as well as plotters and a few other devices. However, some printers and other equipment use an RS232C serial port instead. My printers and plotters have both types of port built-in as standard, and there seems to be a definite trend towards this dual standard.

A parallel port differs from a serial type in that it uses eight connecting wires to transfer data from the computer to the printer. It therefore transfers data a byte at a time, whereas a serial type sends data (literally) bit-by-bit. A parallel interface is generally much faster than even the highest speed serial type, but in many cases the slowness of the peripheral which receives the data will make this irrelevant. Long connecting cables are permissible with serial links, but with parallel types proper operating is only guaranteed over cables of 2 metres or less in length. Note that a parallel port is only an output type, and, unlike a serial type, it is not to be used to feed data into the computer. You may occasionally come across references to bidirectional parallel ports, but this is a bit misleading. Ports of this type can be set to operate as an input type for specialist applications, but they can not be used simultaneously as an input port and an output type.

CGA
This stands for "colour graphics adaptor", and it is a type of screen display adaptor for IBM PCs and compatibles. It provides 640 x 200 pixel resolution in monochrome, and 320 x 200 pixel resolution in four colours (which includes the background colour).

CISC
This is an acronym for Comprehensive (or Complete or Complicated) Instruction Set Chip. This describes the currently most popular type of microprocessor, which has a large number of instructions, as distinct from the reduced instruction set chips (RISC).

CLI
CLI is an acronym for "command line interpreter". This normally refers to an operating system where the commands are typed in at the keyboard (as with MS-DOS and CP/M) rather than using a WIMP environment (like GEM for example).

Clock
All computers have a simple electronic circuit which generates electrical pulses at a regular rate, and this is the "clock". The clock frequency is usually controlled by a quartz crystal (as used in watches, etc.). The clock controls the rate at which the computer functions. The faster the clock, the faster the computer runs. You can not speed up a computer simply by raising its clock frequency, as the microprocessor, memory circuits, etc. have a strict limit on their maximum operating speed. Most computers are run at a clock speed very close to the maximum at which the various pieces of hardware are guaranteed to still operate reliably. More than marginally raising the clock speed is almost certain to cause a malfunction. The clock rate is normally specified in megahertz (MHz), and 1MHz is one million pulses per second. Note that the number of instructions the microprocessor performs per second is not normally equal to the number of clock cycles per second. Complex instructions on some microprocessors take more than twenty clock cycles to complete.

Comms
This is an abbreviation of "communications". A comms program is one which simplifies the use of a modem by setting up the necessary baud rates and protocols, and which will also have other facilities such as auto-dial and auto-answer.

Compatible
There is a popular computer joke about the dictionary definition of "compatible", which should be something like "unique and totally unlike anything else on the market". This is perhaps a gross exaggeration, but is not totally untrue. Manufacturers can not produce an exact copy of an existing product, or even a very close copy, for obvious legal reasons. It is quite alright to produce a product that will emulate another one, provided it works in a slightly different way to the original. However, by working in a different manner it is virtually inevitable that any emulation product is going to be less than fully compatible. Compatible is a term that is mainly applied to the so-called "clones" of the IBM PC range of computers. Most modern "clones" are very compatible, and there are few programs (if any) that will not run properly on the average "clone". However, if you use an IBM compatible computer it is always a good idea to check that a program will run on it properly before actually buying it.

Compiler
Programming languages such as normal versions of BASIC are interpreted languages. In other words, when the program is run the computer takes each BASIC instruction, converts it into a machine code routine that the microprocessor can run, and then runs that routine. This system of interpreting each line as the program progresses can be very slow, with

the interpreting taking longer than it takes the machine code routines to run. In fact it can often take a hundred or even a thousand times longer for each instruction to be interpreted than it does for the resultant machine code routine to execute. It is this factor that makes interpreted languages relatively slow in operation. A compiler does things in a different way. A completed program is first compiled into a machine code program, or a sort of pseudo machine code that needs minimal interpretation, and then it is run. This gives very much faster operation. There are drawbacks to compiled languages, one of which is that they still tend to be relatively expensive to buy. The main drawback is simply that they generally give the programmer less help than interpreted languages. This makes program writing more difficult, especially for beginners.

Composite Video

This is a standard for sending the VDU output from a computer to the monitor. It allows all the necessary signals for intensity and (where appropriate) colour to be sent using a single wire (with earth return). Many computers have a composite video output, but currently it is losing ground to analogue RGB and RGBI type outputs, which allow a slightly better picture quality, in theory at least.

Co-Ordinates

In drawing graphics on a computer system, some system of specifying where lines and points are to be placed is necessary. In order to do this, the screen or other drawing surface is treated rather like a sheet of graph paper, with a grid of horizontal and vertical lines, though the lines are never visible. Points can then be specified by giving their displacement in terms of horizontal and vertical offsets on the imaginary grid. These offsets are the co-ordinates of the point, and are usually given relative to the *graphics origin*, which is the point with co-ordinates 0, 0. Usually the graphics origin is the bottom left-hand corner of the drawing surface, but in some cases it may be placed in the centre of the screen (this is usual with graphics in the LOGO language). Some systems allow the graphics origin to be placed anywhere on the drawing surface the user requires. When the graphics origin is in the bottom left-hand corner, only positive co-ordinates are required. In all other cases, co-ordinates can be either positive or negative.

When drawing on the screen, a co-ordinate system where the units correspond to the actual screen is sometimes used. This is termed *pixel co-ordinates*. However, it is now common to use a system where the increments of the co-ordinate system are much smaller than the screen pixels. This makes it possible to transfer graphics from the screen to a device (such as a plotter) with a higher resolution, and make full use of this extra potential.

Context Switching

Context switching is similar to multi-tasking in that it is a system which allows two or more application programs to be in memory simultaneously. Unlike multi-tasking, however, only one program at a time is actually running, the others being held in a state of suspension. It is possible, however, to quickly switch from one program to another, usually without having to save the work you have done to disc (this may be done automatically). Context switching avoids much of the complication of multi-tasking, but allows a computer user to move much more readily from one job to another than is the case if programs have to be loaded and run from disc. It is a system which deserves to be used much more widely than it is. Perhaps the best-known context switching system is the in-built software in the Cambridge Computers Z88 portable computer.

Co-Processor

Some computers (notably the BBC model B series) have the ability to take add-on boards which have a different microprocessor to the one fitted in the computer. With this board (or external co-processor unit) activated, its microprocessor effectively takes over from the one in the computer. The idea of a co-processor is to increase the processing power of the computer, or to provide compatibility with an operating system which requires a microprocessor other than the one fitted in the computer. For example, the BBC model B series of computers are fitted with a 6502 microprocessor, but with the Z80 co-processor fitted they can run the CP/M operating system. Do not confuse a co-processor with a maths co-processor, which is a very different concept (see MATHS CO-PROCESSOR).

CP/M

This is a disc operating system for 8 bit personal computers. Although it is regarded by many as obsolete, there are a large number of computers running under this system in use today. CP/M has had something of a renaissance due to the popularity of the Amstrad 8 bit computers which can run under this operating system. There is a vast range of software available for use on CP/M machines, and it is possible to obtain CP/M emulators for MS-DOS computers and some other computers (the Atari ST range for example). The idea of these emulation programs is not usually to provide a means of setting up a 16 bit system to run exclusively under CP/M. It is more a matter of providing existing CP/M users with a means of running their existing programs on more modern hardware while making the transition to using more modern equipment. Emulation programs in general run rather slowly, and a powerful 16 bit computer running a CP/M emulation program might operate more slowly than an 8 bit machine designed for CP/M use! Running CP/M on a 16 bit is not necessarily a means of obtaining a "turbo" performance CP/M system.

CPS

This stands for "characters per second", and is a measure of how fast a printer can produce text. Some manufacturers are reasonably honest about the speed of their printers, but many quote speeds obtained under the most favourable possible settings and conditions, and seem to have longer seconds than the rest of us!

CPU

This stands for "central processing unit", and it is perhaps better known these days as a microprocessor. This is the component at the heart of a micro-computer, which controls everything, does all the calculating, etc. Actually most computers have special components which handle functions such as graphics and sound with a minimum of information being supplied by the microprocessor. This reduces the workload on the microprocessor and generally results in programs running faster. The fact that two different computers are based on the same CPU does not, therefore, mean that they are equal in terms of computing power.

Cursor

With most programs where you input data onto the screen there is an on-screen character which indicates where the next piece of data will appear. In the case of the word processor I am using to produce this, for example, it is a short line on the screen which flashes on and off a couple of times per second. This on-screen character is the cursor. There is an alternative but little used meaning, and this is for a device (such as a mouse) which is used to control the position of the cursor.

Daisy-Wheel

This is a term used to describe a type of printer. It has a sort of wheel with numerous spokes, and the type-faces are at the ends of these spokes. In operation the wheel spins so that the required character is at the top, and a hammer mechanism then presses it against the ribbon and paper. This type of printer can produce superb results, especially if it is used with a carbon ribbon. There are drawbacks to daisy-wheel printers though, which are mostly quite noisy, slow (only about 10 to 20 cps in most cases), and are not really suitable for graphics use. They have waned in popularity somewhat in recent years, probably due to the improvements in the various types of dot-matrix printer.

Data

Data simply means any stored information. Almost any type of computer generated file can be termed a data file, with the exception of stored programs. The term is most commonly used to describe files generated by database and spreadsheet programs, but is by no means exclusive to these. In the BASIC language, DATA is a keyword which indicates to the interpreter that what follows on the program line is constant data for use by the program when running.

Database

I suppose that any store of information could be termed a database. It is generally taken to mean a large store of information stored in an electronic (computer controlled) system that enables any desired piece of data to be easily located and retrieved. There are many programs available that will enable a computer to operate as a database. It is also possible to access enormous databases using a computer plus a modem, but these systems are generally for professional users, and can be quite expensive. On the other hand, they provide almost instant access to vast amounts of information, and can be very worthwhile if a system (or systems) having the right kind of information can be found.

Default

In a colour display, a computer will display a standard set of colours, but it may be possible to change these to others when required. The standard colours are an example of defaults, the action a computer takes unless it is told to do something else. This term has many applications, covering areas such as screen modes, baud rates for communications, which printer port to use, and what character to use for the cursor. On some machines the defaults can be changed to the user's preferred settings either by storing the changes in a special area of memory which is not lost when the machine is switched off (battery backed or non-volatile RAM) or by automatically running a batch file on switch-on.

The term can also be applied to peripheral devices such as printers. Printers will default to a particular print size, style and character set at switch-on, and these defaults can be altered by software commands or by controls on the printer. Often the default on printers can be changed by control switches, or on more recent ones by EEPROM.

Digitiser

A digitiser is a sort of electronic drawing board which connects to the computer. It is used to control the cursor, very much like using a mouse. However, the cursor is controlled using a sort of electronic pen, and placing this on the drawing board sets the cursor to the equivalent point on the screen. Digitisers are mainly used with computer aided drawing (CAD) and paint programs. They can be used to trace over existing drawings and load them into the computer. Many programs that operate with a digitiser have a menu overlay that is placed on the drawing board, and the pen is then used for menu selection to control the program. In some cases the alphabet is included on the overlay, and even text is entered from the digitiser instead of from the keyboard!

An image digitiser or video digitiser is an electronic device which takes a signal from a video camera, video recorder, or broadcast TV signal and converts it to a digital form which can be displayed on a computer screen, and also modified by a drawing program. Such devices can be very expensive, but simpler and moderately priced systems intended for the home user are available.

Directory

This is a list of files and sub-directories on a disc. From MS-DOS a directory can be displayed on the screen simply by typing the DIRectory command (e.g. "DIR A: RETURN" to list the files and sub-directories on the disc in drive A:). Some other operating systems use CAT (catalogue) instead. Apart from telling what is on a disc, this command will also tell you how much unused space is available on the disc.

Disc (Disk)

This is the all-important device used for storing programs and data. There are a range of disc sizes from 2.8 inches to 8 inches. The 8 inch discs are now obsolete, although there is still a great deal of equipment fitted with this size of disc still in use. The 5.25 inch discs are probably the most common type, although the 3.5 inch type have now become the standard, and in the fullness of time should become the only type of disc in use. The 3 inch discs are not used on many computers, but they are still quite common due to their use on the very popular Amstrad 8 bit machines. The 2.8 inch discs were designed for use with electronic musical instruments such as sound samplers, and do not seem to have been used in other applications.

The discs are coated with a magnetic material, and data is recorded onto them in a fashion that is essentially the same as conventional tape recording. The advantage of a disc over a tape system is that it is easy for the disc drive to jump to any part of the disc almost instantly (so called "random access"). A tape system has to wind backwards or forwards through a tape until it comes to the required section, which can be very slow indeed. A disc is formatted into a number of tracks, and each track is divided into sectors. The 360k IBM standard discs have 40 tracks on each side of the disc, and 9 sectors per track. This gives 360 sectors on each side of the disc, 720 sectors in total, and with each one providing 0.5k of storage this gives a capacity of 360k.

You will sometimes find references to 500k and 1M discs, which in fact only seem to have capacities of 360k and 720k respectively. The discrepancy arises due to the amount of disc space taken up by the formatting process. Discs are normally supplied in unformatted form, and you have to format them prior to use. The formatting process lays down the basic framework of the tracks and sectors, and also provides the basic framework for the directory. This is part of the disc which stores information about

what is on the disc, and just where it is on the disc. When you access a file on a disc, the operating system uses this information to find out where the required file is stored, and it can then quickly jump to the appropriate sectors of the disc. An arrangement of this type is essential if the potential speed of a disc system is to be fully realised.

There are a variety of disc formats in common use, as some discs have 40 tracks per side while others have 80. Some discs are single-sided while others use both sides of the disc. There are also single and double density drives (actually it is the disc interface rather than the drive which squeezes twice as much data onto each sector of the disc). You can sometimes read a disc using a drive and interface of the wrong type, but this is not usually possible. You may also be able to get away with using a blank disc of the wrong type provided it is formatted correctly for your disc drive. Single-sided discs always seem to have the magnetic coating on both sides – they are not guaranteed to be usable on the second side. You may get away with using single-sided discs in a double-sided drive, but the small saving in cost would hardly seem to justify the increased risk of lost data. There is no risk in using a disc which is over-specified, such as using an 80 track type in a 40 track drive. This should actually give marginally improved reliability, but the discs will cost more of course.

There are high density ("HD") discs in both the 5.25 and 3.5 inch sizes. These are 80 track types, but they are used in drives which cram a large amount of data onto each track. The 5.25 inch high density discs have a capacity of about 1.6 megabytes, leaving a formatted capacity of about 1.2 megabytes. Ordinary 40 and 80 track discs will not give good reliability if used with a high density disc drive. Only use the proper high density discs of good quality with these drives.

A hard disc is basically the same as ordinary 5.25 inch floppy types, and is used to magnetically store and retrieve data. The disc is built into the disc drive, and is not removable and interchangeable like floppy discs. For this reason the alternative term of "fixed disc" is sometimes used. This type of disc and drive is highly refined, and can usually save and load data at least ten times faster than a good floppy disc. Unlike a floppy disc, the disc rotates all the time the computer is switched on. This avoids any waiting while the discs gets up to the correct rotation speed. This is important as the disc (which in practice is actually several discs stacked one above the other) is relatively heavy, and rotates at a relatively high speed. It consequently takes it much longer than a floppy disc to get up to full speed. The recording and play-back heads are aerodynamic so that they fly over the disc and never come into contact with it. Due to the high disc speed the consequences of a head coming into contact with the disc would apparently be catastrophic.

The storage capacity of a hard disc is many times higher than that of a floppy disc at around 10 to 100 megabytes or even more (which compares with about 0.36 megabytes for an average floppy disc). Thus, the fact that the disc is not interchangeable is not a great disadvantage. They may be called hard discs, but they are certainly not hardy discs. They must be treated with due respect if they are to give many years of trouble-free service. They are sometimes more expensive than the computer they are used with, but they are often worth the expense as much of the best software available will only work really well on a machine equipped with a hard disc.

Dot Matrix

This normally refers to a printer which has (most commonly) 9 pins in the print head. The printed characters are made up from patterns of dots, and when used in the high-speed "draft" mode these dots are usually quite visible. Most dot matrix printers also have a higher quality NLQ (near letter quality) mode where each line of characters is printed twice, with the paper being moved up fractionally on the second run. This sort of merges the dots together, but does not necessarily disguise them completely. It substantially reduces the printing speed. Dot matrix printers are the most popular type, and offer great versatility including good graphics capability. Reasonably priced 24 pin types have now been introduced, and these offer higher print quality while still maintaining a fairly high print speed. Where high quality is of prime importance, daisy wheel printers (which work in a manner more like a conventional typewriter) still represent the better choice. Note that ink-jet, laser, and l.e.d. printers all use the same dot method of producing characters. In fact this is essentially the same process that is used to generate characters on a computer's display.

Editor

This is a program for producing and editing text files. It could be regarded as a word processor that has been stripped of all its "frills". In fact some text editors have quite comprehensive features these days, including word-wrap, search and replace, etc. Where they really differ from a word processor is that they have no pagination facilities and have no built-in means of outputting text to a printer. They are intended for such things as producing batch files, and for producing program files for use with an assembler or compiler. Business computers are often supplied with a text editor which is part of the operating system. However, these text editors are often quite crude compared to the best text editors that are available. They are not noted for being particularly easy to use. For most purposes a word processor is much better. An editor can be useful when it is important to produce a pure ASCII file (such as a control file that will be used by a program). Many

word processors add their own brand of formatting codes to the text, and these tend to crash applications programs if you use such a word processor to produce a control file. Some word processors have a facility to produce ASCII files which are free from their formatting codes, but in my experience these do not always give the desired result when used to produce control files for "fussy" programs.

EGA

EGA stands for "enhanced graphics adaptor". This is a display adaptor for IBM PCs and compatibles, and it goes some way beyond the capabilities of the CGA board. It provides resolutions of 640 x 200 pixels in 16 colours, 640 x 350 in monochrome, and 640 x 350 in 16 colours. The full range of colours is only available if the board is fitted with the full 256k of RAM (most EGA boards these days have the full 256k of memory as standard). To obtain the benefits of the EGA display a high resolution monitor having a higher scan rate than the ordinary CGA monitors is required. Apart from its improved graphics capability, the EGA display also provides a much neater text display than the CGA display. The cost of EGA boards and monitors has fallen considerably in recent years, but is still substantially higher than that of CGA equipment.

Emulator

An emulator is a program or a hardware device which allows a computer to act as if it were a different type of computer. The main purpose of this is to allow one machine to run software designed to run on a different machine, or under an alien operating system. Emulators are rarely more than partially successful. Simple software emulators generally run much slower than the machines they emulate, and more complex hardware emulators are often virtually complete computers, only using the host machine's display (and perhaps memory). They can be nearly as expensive as the computer they emulate. See CP/M.

Expert System

This is a relatively new and advanced form of software. It is an extension of CAD (computer aided design). With CAD a computer is used as a design aid, and it will help with the production of a design, and mathematically test the design to predict how well (or otherwise) it will work. An expert system uses so-called artificial intelligence to go on step further. The basic idea is that you tell the system what you want, and then it designs it for you. Systems of this type are not limited to designing though, and are used in medicine and other fields of interest. The point of an expert system is that it enables practically anyone to undertake the type of thing that would normally require someone with years of training and experience behind them. As yet there are relatively few expert systems that really live up to their name.

Extension

See FILE.

Feature

1. An aspect of a computer's or program's specification found in the advertising but not in the instruction manual.
2. A documented bug.

File

If, for instance, you write a letter using a word processor, and then store the letter on disc, the stored data is called a "disc file", or just a "file". If you list the contents of a disc using the MS-DOS DIR instruction, each file will be displayed as a separate entity, together with its file name. Programs of any form of data stored on disc are held in files. MS-DOS file names can have up to eight letters and (or) numbers, and a few other characters are permitted. The three character "extension" is also permitted, and this is separated from the main file name by a full stop. There are certain conventions that are used for program file extensions (".BAS" for a BASIC program for example), but for data files the user can opt for any extension he or she feels is appropriate. Often you can simply omit extensions if you prefer, but a few applications programs insist on having an extension if they are to function properly, and some automatically add one for you!

Flag

In programming, it is sometimes necessary to leave a signal that something has happened so that this can be checked by other parts of the program. This is done by means of flags. At the machine code level, a flag is normally a single specified bit of a particular byte in memory. This can be set or cleared as required, and checked as often as necessary. In higher-level programming (e.g. in BASIC), variables can be used for this purpose.

Floppy Disc

See DISC.

Floppy Tape

This is a rather silly name for a system which uses a continuous loop of tape in a cartridge as a data recording medium. It is intermediate in both speed and cost between floppy discs and audio tape cassettes, has not achieved any great popularity, and should now be considered obsolescent.

Format

Before a disc can be used to store data it must be formatted. This means dividing the disc up into convenient sized blocks and putting down the basic framework of data that will enable the computer to rapidly locate any particular block on the disc, and the data it contains. Formatting is usually carried out via the computer's operating system using the "FORMAT" instruction. With some home computers that were originally designed more for use with cassette tapes than with discs, a separate formatting program may be required. Take due care with formatting commands, as they effectively wipe any data from a disc that has been in use and is accidentally reformatted. Hard disc users need to be especially careful.

The term format can also be used to describe the way in which the data is recorded on the medium. Programs may have their own format for data storage which will prevent data files generated by one program being loaded into another for which they are inappropriate. However, there are also some standard formats expressly designed to allow data to be transferred from one program to another. For example, a model generated on one spreadsheet could be used on another different spreadsheet program, or used by a graphics program to generate graphs or diagrams. When choosing software, it is always worth checking whether new programs can work in conjunction with your existing ones in this way, even if you think you will never need this facility. If you have the ability to swop data between programs you will probably soon find a use for this facility!

Formula

A mathematical expression in a spreadsheet. See FUNCTION.

Frame Grabber

An electronic device which stores a picture from a video camera or recorder, or broadcast TV, in a form suitable for computer storage, display and modification. See also DIGITISER.

Front End

This is the part of a program or operating system with which the operator interacts. WIMP environments such as the Apple Macintosh operating system and GEM are termed "friendly front ends".

Function

A function is a mathematical operation expressed in a computer language. Most computer languages include a number of in-built functions for basic mathematics, and in some languages these can be used together to perform more complex operations. These combinations are called user-defined functions. In compiled languages the functions are usually contained in a 'library' which has to be added to the object code during compilation.

In spreadsheets, functions are called formulas.

Function Keys

These are extra keys provided on many computer keyboards. These do not normally produce on-screen characters, but are used by many applications programs to call up certain functions (f10 might be used to save data to disc for example).

GEM

This is the trade name of the Digital Research operating system front end/graphics system. It is an acronym deriving from Graphics Environment Manager. It is available for many machines, and is supplied as standard with the Atari ST series and the Amstrad PC1512/1640.

Graphics

This means anything which deals with drawings of some kind, instead of being purely text based. Most graphics programs include text, but the text characters are normally defined by the applications programs and are not the normal (text screen) text characters. Some text programs are actually graphics types, and this is where various sizes and styles of text are used. These can not be handled by a normal text screen (or printer), and are produced using the graphics capability of the system.

Hard Disc

See DISC.

Hard Copy

This simply refers to a printed copy of a text document, drawing or whatever.

Hard Page

This is a word processing term and refers to a page break which is inserted by the user rather than being inserted automatically by the program, the latter being a "soft page". Soft page breaks will be moved if you add text ahead of them. Hard pages are fixed.

Hard CR (Carriage Return)

This is another word processing term, and refers to a carriage return which is inserted by the user rather than the program. Normally word processing programs automatically take care of carriage returns, automatically beginning a new line where necessary. Hard returns generally only need to be inserted to end paragraphs or to insert extra line spaces in a document.

Hardware

Any piece of equipment in the system (computer, printer, etc.) is a piece of "hardware". Programs are the "software". Software built into the computer and contained on components within the computer is sometimes called the "firmware".

High Level (Language)

A high level computer language is one which makes concessions to human ways of thinking and doing, and is therefore hopefully easy for humans to understand and write. It is especially applied to interpreted languages like BASIC and LOGO.

I/O

I/O simply stands for "input/output". It is generally used in connection with ports such as the RS232C serial port, rather than data stored and retrieved on disc, or something of this type.

Icon

A general term for a graphical representation of something (usually a program or file), displayed on the monitor's screen. A mouse or other pointing device is used to select the desired icon, rather than typing in a program name, file name, or whatever. This is the system used when running GEM desktop.

Indirection

In machine code, an instruction may contain an address in memory, and this address in memory will in turn contain the address at which the data to be used by the instruction will be found. This process is termed indirection. In theory, an infinite number of stages of indirection are possible, but in fact in microprocessors true indirection is hardly ever implemented, largely because it is very greedy of stack space. Instead, register indirection is normally used, where an address register in the microprocessor is specified in the instruction and is used to contain the address of the data. Indirection is most commonly used when accessing tables of data in memory. The register containing the address can be incremented or decremented to step through the table.

Ink-Jet

This is a type of printer which forms characters in the standard dot-matrix format. However, instead of having a 9 or 24 pin print-head and a ribbon, they work by squirting minuscule droplets of ink from the print-head. They can give very good quality, are very fast, extremely quiet, and the modern types are very reliable. The cost is substantially more than that of a good dot matrix printer, but they can be worthwhile for those who will make extensive use of their printer. This type of printer is incapable of producing carbon copies, and this will rule them out for some applications.

Instruction

A machine code program consists of a series of instructions. Each instruction consists of an opcode and an operand or operand field. These terms are explained below. However, in some cases an instruction can consist of an opcode alone.

Interface

The original meaning of "interface" was a port, such as a Centronics or RS232C type, that enabled two items of equipment to be interconnected. This is still its primary meaning, but you may also encounter this term in the context of a so-called "user interface". This is the means by which the user interacts with the computer, and GEM desktop is an example of a user interface.

Interpreter

A program which is the key part of a programming language. When a program written in an interpreted language is run, the interpreter scans the program line by line, determines what needs to be done, and does it. This process is necessarily slow (by computing standards) but programs in interpreted languages have the advantage that they are easily modified and tested. See also COMPILER.

Interrupts

There are various hardware devices within and attached to computers which periodically need to grab a share of the microprocessor's attention. They do this by putting a signal on a special pin on the MPU chip. This signal causes the MPU to suspend its current activity, to store all necessary information so that it can resume where it left off (usually on the stack), and then to branch to a special section of code in memory which contains the instructions to service the peripheral device. This process is termed an interrupt and the code is called the interrupt routine. Most microcomputers run under continuous interrupts, but since each interrupt only takes a small fraction of a second to service, the user is not aware of this.

Justification

This is a word processing term, and refers to the process whereby the margins are made even down the length of the document. The left margin normally is justified as the text lines start from the left margin, but the right margin will be ragged as the lines will be of differing length. The right margin can also be justified, and the simplest way of doing this is by inserting extra spaces between words. This can be done on-screen and in the printed document. A better system is micro-space justification, where extra space is placed between letters within words, as well as between words. This gives a neater appearance to the document, but is not possible with all printers. It requires a high degree of co-ordination between printer and program. Word processors employing microspacing justification do not usually justify on-screen. For some purposes, justification is undesirable, so there is nearly always provision for turning it off.

Right-only justification is also provided in some cases. Here, the lines are not padded out, but are shifted right to justify them, leaving the left margin ragged.

You may also come across centre justification. In this, lines are not padded at all. Each line is centred so that it has equal space either end, but both margins are ragged. This is not a true form of justification.

Keyed File

This is a system of organising database files, whereby each entry in the file also has entries in one or more index files. These work just like the index in a book.

When looking for a record in the file, the part of the record you specify is looked up in the appropriate index, and the record or records which match your specification are thus located. Keyed files allow very rapid file location, but take up a lot of disc space as both the data file and the indexes have to be stored. A very few versions of BASIC allow users to write their own keyed file programs.

Kilobyte (Kbyte or k)

This simply means one thousand bytes, or if you want to be pedantic, it actually means 1024 bytes. It is the most convenient unit for expressing the size of computer memory (RAM and ROM) and disc capacity.

LAN

LAN stands for "local area network". This means connecting computers together effectively for one large system which can share software, swop data, share peripherals such as printers, etc.

Laser Printer

A LASER printer is based on photocopier technology, but a laser beam is used to generate a page of printing/graphics. This gives very high quality output with each page being produced very rapidly (typically about eight pages per second). Very nice if you can afford one! Like ink-jet printers, carbon copies are not possible, but the speed of laser printers makes the production of multiple copies a practical proposition.

LCD

In a computer context this generally applies to the screen of a portable computer. LCD stands for "liquid crystal display", and it is the same technology that is used in the displays of watches, calculators, etc. Early liquid crystal displays for computer use were often small and low in quality. More recent types are generally larger, display more information, and are much clearer.

LED

The main use of LEDs (light emitting diodes) is in displays, but they are little used in computer applications. In a computing context you are more likely to encounter the term as a description of a printer. LED printers are very similar to laser types, but use a LED light source instead of a laser.

Library

In computing the term library is used mostly in the context of programming. In compiling languages, the library is a collection of complex machine code routines which perform the more involved mathematical operations and similar tasks. With the better compilers, only the parts of a library actually required by a program are added to it. In simpler compilers, the entire library is always added. This means that the programs written with such a compiler will always be larger than they need to be. Unfortunately, most compilers are of the latter type. Libraries can also cause complications if programs in a compiling language are being written for commercial sale. The library routines will be the copyright of the producer of the compiler, and a licence may be required to sell programs containing them. With some languages, additional libraries can be obtained, extending the language's capabilities in such areas as graphics.

In programming in languages such as BASIC, the term library is usually used to mean a collection of subroutines or procedures of a general purpose nature which are kept on disc and which can be merged into any program one is writing which needs them.

List

This term is used in languages such as LISP and LOGO, which are list processing languages (LISP is in fact derived from LISt Processing). They are the primary form of data storage in these languages. A list is a collection of words, which in fact can be any collection of one or more printable characters. It is possible in these languages to add words to either end of a list, to remove words from either end of a list, and to transfer words from one list to another. There are also functions to determine whether a word is a member of a list, the position of a word in a list and so on. It is also possible to have a list of lists, a list of lists of lists, and so on (theoretically) *ad infinitum.* These facilities may seem limited, but in fact a great deal can be done with them, and these languages form the basis of artificial intelligence research.

Low Level (Language)

A low level language is one which makes few concessions to humans and keeps close to the requirements of the machine. It is most often used to mean machine code or assembly language.

Mac

This is an affectionate abbreviation of the popular Apple Macintosh computer, one of the original WIMP machines, and certainly the one which made graphical front ends a success.

Machine Code
See ASSEMBLER.

Mainframe

A mainframe computer is a very powerful type, generally capable of carrying out many tasks at once with many users. Equivalent in power to a larger number of microcomputers in fact.

Maths Co-Processor

Some computers, including most IBM PC/XT/AT and compatible machines, have a socket on the main printed circuit board for a maths co-processor. This is an integrated circuit which looks very much the same as the microprocessor in most cases. Its purpose is to aid the microprocessor by taking over and handling the calculations when floating point and other intensive calculations must be performed. Maths co-processors are very complex devices, and have prices that are generally between about £100.00 and £500.00. This may seem rather expensive, but they can provide a very worthwhile improvement in performance. Just how much of an improvement depends on the software in use. Most maths co-processors will only operate with software that is written to take advantage of them. Some programs are supplied in two versions − one for use with computers that are fitted with a maths co-processor, and one for use with computers that lack this facility. A maths co-processor can be of little benefit with programs that do not make extensive use of complex mathematical calculations. A maths co-processor will not speed up a word processor for example. They are of most benefit with software such as spreadsheets and CAD programs. The effect of one of these components is to speed up certain types of calculation by a factor of fifty or more. However, this does not mean that adding one will speed up a spreadsheet or CAD program by this amount. Probably no practical applications programs are pure mathematical calculations. The speed-up can be very worthwhile though, and adding a maths co-processor might speed up many parts of a CAD program by a factor of about three. The exact boost in performance is very much program dependent though.

Megabyte (Mbyte or M)

This is a million bytes, or a thousand kilobytes. To be precise, it is actually 1048576 bytes, or 1024 kilobytes. This unit is becoming more useful to express memory size, as many computers are now becoming available with memories in this range. It is also the most convenient unit to express the storage capacity of hard discs.

Memory

A computer's memory is the circuit where it stores programs and data. Some of this is the system firmware which boots the operating system at start-up amongst other things. For the user it is the RAM (random access memory) that is of more interest. This is used to store any programs or data that are fed into the computer, and there must be enough RAM available. Eight bit computers are normally restricted to 64k of normal RAM. Although this seemed to be a massive amount not so long ago, it is very restrictive these days. Many 8 bit computers have some form of "paged" RAM which enables virtually any amount of RAM to be accommodated. This is done by switching between banks of RAM so that no more than 64k is active at any one time. The microprocessor provides no support for this type of extended RAM though, and this tends to make it rather difficult to use, slow in operation, and prone to crashing the system. If carried out properly, this system can work remarkably well though.

Sixteen bit computers can mostly take much larger amounts of memory. 1 megabyte is normally the minimum limit, and many sixteen bit microprocessors can handle sixteen megabytes or more of RAM. The only problem with this is that in practice most computers do not have such large amounts of RAM fitted (which would be rather expensive). Where a really large program is to be used, a common technique is to use program overlays. In other words, much of the program is left on disc and not loaded into the computer. If a function that requires part of the program which has not been loaded should be called, this part of the program is loaded into memory. It then overwrites part of the program already in RAM. If the overwritten part of the program is needed at a later time, it must be read back into memory from disc again. Some programs use a similar method to enable them to deal with data files that are too large to be fully loaded into RAM. In order to work well these systems need the speed and higher capacity of a hard disc. With a program that makes extensive use of overlays there can be an advantage in having a fast access (40ms or less) hard disc.

Memory Resident

This is a type of program, and it is one which when it is run, lays dormant in memory. It can then be invoked by pressing a certain combination of keys. The idea is to run memory resident programs from within other programs. You could, for example, have a memory resident calculator that could be called up at any time, such as when word processing, and then put back into dormant mode when you have finished your calculations. Although memory resident programs are a very good idea, and can be invaluable, there can be problems in using them. There can be clashes between memory resident programs and main applications programs, leading to crashes of the computer. A lot of applications programs are so complex these days that they often use up practically every byte of memory. Programs of this type (which includes virtually all the programs I use) can not be used in conjunction with memory resident programs as there is simply not enough memory available to accommodate all the programs.

Menu

Where a program presents the user with a series of possible options, one way of choosing the required option would be to remember the right key to press. This can be difficult, especially when first using a system when there might be dozens of key codes to remember. Many programs provide a simple help screen with a list of functions and the appropriate key or keys to press in order to obtain each one. This is a sort of menu system, but with a proper menu it is merely a matter of using the mouse or cursor keys to position the cursor alongside the required function. This function is then selected by "clicking" the mouse or pressing RETURN on the keyboard.

Microcomputer (Micro)

A microcomputer is simply a computer that is based on a microprocessor. Virtually all personal and home computers are of this type.

MIDI

MIDI is an acronym for "Musical Instruments Digital Interface". It is a form of serial interface used to send data from one electronic musical instrument to another, or as a means of communication between a computer and one or more electronic instruments. A few computers have a built-in MIDI interface (the Atari ST series for example), and it is an add-on which is available for any of the more popular home and personal computers. It is similar to a standard RS232C interface, and the common word format of one start bit, eight data bits, one stop bit, and no parity is used. However, the baud rate is nonstandard and quite high at 31250 baud, and MIDI uses a 5 milliamp current loop signal rather than the two voltage levels of the RS232C system. Consequently, an RS232C interface can not be used for MIDI purposes unless it can accommodate the higher baud rate and a simple interface box is used to provide the necessary changes in the input/output signals. This is the normal method of MIDI interfacing used for the Commodore Amiga computer, but most other add-on MIDI interfaces connect to the expansion bus of the computer.

Minicomputer

Strictly speaking a minicomputer is a somewhat cutdown and less powerful version of a mainframe computer. As the top notch microcomputers become ever more powerful the distinction between these and minicomputers becomes less clear cut. Probably the most sophisticated microcomputers will gradually take over from minicomputers.

Modem

The term modem is a contraction of "MODulator/DEModulator". It is a device which enables two computer systems to communicate via the telephone lines. It operates by converting the signals from the computer's serial port into two audio tones, and converting received tones back into RS232C serial signals. Direct coupled types are connected direct to the telephone system, and acoustically coupled types send and receive signals via an ordinary telephone handset (see ACOUSTIC COUPLER).

Modulator

An electronic device which converts the video output of a computer (the signal to drive a monitor) into a form suitable to drive a domestic TV via the aerial socket. Picture quality obtained from this system is normally markedly inferior to that obtained from a proper monitor.

MSDOS

This is currently the main operating system for 16 bit computers. It is mainly used with IBM compatible computers (the very similar PCDOS is the operating system normally used on the IBM PCs themselves). There is a vast amount of software that is designed to run under this operating system, and this enables MS-DOS machines to be used in a vast range of applications. In fact there are probably more programs available for these machines than any others.

Multi-Tasking

It is possible to obtain software that enables a computer to undertake several tasks simultaneously. What is really happening is that the computer spends a short time doing one task, then moves on to the next one for a short while, and so on. This can work well because computers do not normally work flat out all the time. For example, when word processing the computer spends most of its time waiting for the next character to be typed rather than actually printing characters on the screen or manipulating the text in some way. Multi-tasking inevitably means that the computer runs each application more slowly than normal, and if two or three applications put heavy demands on the computer simultaneously things can grind along very slowly. (See also CONTEXT SWITCHING and RESIDENT)

Multi-User (System)

Multi-tasking should not be confused with multi-user systems. They are similar in that the computer is time-shared, but with a multi-user system there are several users, each with their own keyboard and monitor. Multi-user systems were originally based on minicomputers and mainframes, but there are microcomputer based systems. The relative cheapness and lower power of microcomputers makes this type of system a less attractive proposition than it is with mini and mainframe types. It is possible to have a system which is both multi-user and multi-tasking.

Numeric Keypad

This is a calculator style keyboard which is included on many computer keyboards, usually towards the right-hand end of the keyboard. On some computers these keys are also used for cursor control and similar purposes. These keys are duplicating functions available on the top row of the standard "QWERTY" typewriter part of the keyboard, but the numeric keypad can be much more convenient for applications that require a larger amount of numeric data to be entered into the computer.

Object Code

In a machine code program produced using an assembler or compiler, the object code is the machine code output produced by the assembler or compiler.

Object Oriented

This is a term which is normally applied to drawing programs. Paint type programs are pixel oriented, which means that the drawing is produced by altering the pixels on the screen of the monitor, and it is stored as a simple bit map of the screen display. This is a very simple way of handling things which is adequate for many purposes, but it has disadvantages. One of these is that the resolution of most computer displays, even the higher resolution types such as the IBM EGA display, have what is by normal standards a rather poor level of resolution. Output devices such as printers and plotters are normally capable of a much higher resolution output than the screen. With the image only stored at the screen resolution, it can only be output to the printer or plotter at this resolution, giving what are often disappointing results. Some recent paint programs have routines which try to smooth out the steps in curves and diagonal lines when hard-copy is produced, but usually results are still some way short of the best that can be achieved by the output device.

CAD programs use a different approach. They store the drawings in terms of objects, such as lines, circles, text etc. Details of each object's size, position, etc. are stored in very high resolution form. Most CAD programs will accept dimensions into the tens of thousands, with about half a dozen decimal places being permitted if desired. In terms of pixel resolution, the drawing may well be stored on the basis of a few billion pixels on each axis, and countless billions of pixels in total. Of course, the drawing can not be displayed on screen in anything like this resolution, and the program simply provides the best possible on-screen representation that can be produced. In fact the same is true whatever the output device, and the accuracy of the hard-copy from a CAD program will normally be limited by the output device rather than the program, no matter how good the output device happens to be.

Which type of program is best depends on the application. An artist would feel rather restricted by a CAD program, and would feel more at home with the freedom and "tricks" afforded by most paint programs. A draftsman would feel severely hampered by the lack of accuracy provided by a paint program, and would have little use for the "spraycans" etc. of a paint program. An important advantage of CAD programs and their object orientation is that single objects, or a group of objects can be selected and then manipulated in some way. The usual facilities are such things as scaling, rotating, stretching, etc. With pixel oriented programs the same sort of things are usually possible, but these facilities work on an area of the screen rather than specific objects, which does not always give the desired effect.

Opcode

The opcode is the part of a complete instruction in machine code which directs the CPU to perform a specific task. It normally comes at the beginning of the complete instruction. In some cases, instructions may consist of an opcode alone.

Operand

The majority of instructions in a machine code program will contain, in addition to the opcode, either some data on which the instruction is to operate, or the memory location where data is to be found or placed, or more than one of these. This part of the instruction is termed the operand. The term operand field is also used, meaning the part of the instruction containing the operand. Some instructions do not require an operand, and in some others it is implicit.

Operating System

The main point about an operating system such as MS-DOS is that it effectively turns the computer into a standard machine which will run any software intended for that particular operating system. This enables different computers to run the same software. In practice things are not quite as straight forward as this, and there can be compatibility problems. Software that controls the computer's input/output devices via the operating system can run rather slowly. Many programs use direct control to some extent in order to speed things up. Programs of this type are to some extent hardware specific, and simply having the right operating system does not guarantee that they will run properly. Another point to bear in mind is that to run some programs properly the system must include extra memory or other hardware which goes beyond the specification of most computers that use the operating system concerned. An operating system therefore only offers conditional software compatibility.

An operating system also enables useful tasks such as disc formatting, disc copying etc. to be carried out, and it is not just needed to enable applications programs to be run.

ORing

See BITWISE.

OS/2

This is a relatively new operating system from Microsoft (the company that is also responsible for the industry standard MS-DOS operating system). OS/2 requires an 80286 or 80386 based computer (8088 and 8086 based machines are unsuitable) and it provides multi-tasking. In other words, it provides the ability to run more than one program at a time. It requires a lot of memory though (1 megabyte for the operating system alone). It is still early days for

this operating system, but it looks very much as though it will become dominant in the 1990s.

Overlay

In very large programs, if the whole of the program is loaded into memory at once, there may not be enough memory space left for the storage and manipulation of data. In such cases, some lesser used parts of the program may not be loaded into memory when the program is first loaded. They are only loaded from disc if actually required, when they overwrite part of the program already in memory. If the overwritten part is subsequently required, it must be reloaded. Sections of program loaded on demand like this are called overlays. When using a program which has overlays it is often necessary to leave the program disc in the drive all the time the program is running. Such programs are difficult to use unless you either have a two-drive computer or are running from a hard disc.

Paint Program

Paint programs is the name generally given to pixel-orientated drawing programs. These allow pictures to be drawn on the screen, normally using a mouse, and provide facilities for lines, circles, boxes and other shapes to be drawn and, if required, filled with colour or patterns. Freehand drawing is also supported, and there are facilities to move, copy, and "flip" (duplicate as a mirror image) parts of the drawn picture. The picture is stored only in screen memory, and can not be scaled up or down. Programs of this sort are used mostly for recreational purposes or for producing screen images for use in conjunction with games programs. They are generally not suited to serious technical applications. However, some word processing programs allow pictures produced with compatible paint programs to be included in documents.

Pal

This is the standard used for colour TV transmission in the U.K. and most of the rest of Western Europe with the exception of France. It stands for Phase Alternate Line.

Parallel Interface

See CENTRONICS INTERFACE.

Parallel Processing

A system of computing whereby a number of microprocessors work on a task at once, that is, in parallel, allowing very fast processing. This system is as yet very little used, but has enormous potential if it can be effectively implemented.

Parsing

In an interpreted language, during program execution, the interpreter must scan each line in order to determine what action it must take. In the case of lines containing mathematical expressions, several scans of the line may be necessary in order to work out the correct order in which the operations must be performed, according to the rules of operator precedence. This process of scanning a line is called parsing. It is also sometimes used to describe the process of an assembler or compiler scanning the source code in order to assemble or compile it.

PC-DOS

PC-DOS is the operating system used in IBM personal computers, and it is largely compatible with MS-DOS software. The two are not totally compatible, but most programs are available in MS-DOS versions rather than as PC-DOS programs aimed specifically at the IBM personal computers.

Peripheral

A general term for any hardware add-on for a computer (printer, plotter, modem, etc.).

Pipelining

This is a term used in multi-tasking systems when the output of one program is used *directly* as the input to another program running concurrently. Generally this is implemented by the use of areas of memory designated as buffers. If output of one program is sent to another by means of disc files (including RAM disc files) this does not count as pipelining, but is usually termed importing and exporting. True pipelining is very rarely found on microcomputers.

Pixel

This term is derived from "picture element" and refers to the individual points which make up the VDU screen image. The size of a pixel therefore sets the size of the smallest detail which can be displayed. Screen resolution is usually given in pixels, so that a resolution of 640 x 350 means that 640 points can be resolved horizontally by 350 vertically, provided of course that the monitor is good enough.

Pixel Oriented

See OBJECT ORIENTED.

Plotter

A plotter is a device that, under computer control, draws out diagrams on paper or film using a pen. It is a sort of mechanical draftsman! The main uses of plotters are for producing business graphics and technical drawings. For business graphics the plotter is normally armed with fibre-tip pens of various colours and plotting paper or transparency film. For technical drawing the pens are something very similar to conventional technical pens, and the paper is normally some form of tracing paper or drafting film. The drawings in this book were produced using a Roland DXY980A plotter. Although plotters are a rather odd mixture of microprocessor technology, pulley-wheels, and wires, they can produce superb drawings and business graphics. Unfortunately, they

remain very much more expensive than most printers, and large high resolution types can cost many thousands of pounds. They are of little use as text printers as they are very slow (typically around one character per second), but they are designed specifically for drawing purposes and nothing else.

Pointer

In WIMP environments, the pointer is the on-screen symbol, usually an arrow or hand, which is moved by the mouse and is used to point to icons etc.

In programming, a pointer is an address in memory which contains the address of another place in memory where specific data is held. In high-level programming, it can mean a variable which contains the number of an element of an array where specific data is held.

Port

Another general term, and one which describes any electrical connector (plug or socket) on a computer which is used to connect it to other devices. This includes such things as the keyboard socket, and not just things like the serial and parallel interfaces.

Portable

A computer that is fitted with a handle! It is also a term which is used to describe a programming language that has few (if any) differences between various implementations. Few computer languages are truly portable, but C is a language which seems to be more portable than most.

Position Independent Code

A form of machine code program which contains no references to absolute addresses within the program, and which can in consequence run at any position in memory. Some operating systems require all programs to be written in position independent form. This is especially true of multi-tasking and context switching systems.

QWERTY Keyboard

A term which seems to confuse many people, but it simply means a typewriter style keyboard. "QWERTY" is merely the first six letters along the top row of letters keys. The "QWERTY" form is the standard form in the English speaking world, but slight variants are found elsewhere. For example, the "AZERTY" form is found in France and Scandinavia.

RAM

This is a form of memory device, and RAM stands for "random access memory". There is another form of memory called ROM (read only memory). The random access name is a little misleading, in that any part of ROM and RAM banks can be randomly accessed by the computer. The real difference is that the contents of RAM can be altered by the computer, whereas the program or data stored in ROM is put there at the manufacturing stage, and can not be changed. Also, the contents of RAM are lost when the computer is switched off, whereas the contents of ROM devices are retained. RAM is used to store programs and data loaded into the computer, or entered from the keyboard, but any important data must be saved to disc prior to switching off. ROM is used to hold things such as the "boot" routine which loads the operating system from disc when the computer is switched on. In fact, the term random access was originally coined to distinguish this type of memory from "sequential access memory", where the memory can only be read in sequence from the first location to the last. Sequential access memory is no longer used in computers, but it will be found in other electronic devices (e.g. lenses for autofocus SLR cameras).

RAM Disc

If the computer has more memory than an applications program requires, part of RAM can be set aside to act as a sort of pseudo disc drive. This technique is mostly used with programs that use the overlay technique. Storing some of the routines in a RAM disc can make these programs operate very much faster than using a floppy disc to hold the overlays. When using a RAM disc bear in mind that anything stored on this "disc" will be lost when the computer is switched off. This does not matter if the RAM disc is used for program storage, as the program overlays can be loaded from disc each time the system is used. Any data stored in a RAM disc is lost at switch-off though, unless it is copied to a hard or floppy disc.

Random Access File

A random access file is one in which records can be accessed in any sequence, and is distinct from a sequential file in which records can only be accessed in order starting from the first and continuing to the last. Records in random access files normally have to be of a fixed length, and this can be wasteful of disc space, as the length has to be chosen to suit the longest record, and the shorter records padded out. In most random access systems, records are specified by record number, which is the position the record occupies in the file.

Random Number

A truly random number is one which has no reference to any number that has gone before, and has no influence on any number which may follow. In a series of true random numbers, therefore, it is impossible to predict what any number in the sequence will be from others in the sequence. True random numbers are generated in computer systems usually by the use of electronic devices such as noise diodes. The best-known example of this is ERNIE, the computer which generates the numbers of Premium Bonds to be awarded prizes. Most computer languages which provide a random number facility in fact generate pseudo-random numbers, where the numbers do in fact belong to a mathematical series, but where the series is so long and involved that it is very difficult to predict what the next number will be.

Real Time

A much misused term, which really means that the computer is running at precisely the same rate as some event outside the machine. This generally means that it has been deliberately slowed down, but in some very complex tasks a microcomputer has inadequate power to run in real-time. Examples of real time applications would be where the computer is controlling something such as a robot, flight simulation, and processing of an audio signal. Real Time Programming is the branch of programming which deals with control applications and devices, including such things as automatic washing machines and military weapons systems.

Relative Addressing

In a machine code program, relative addressing is a form of addressing in which the address of data or a branch destination is given as a displacement (normally in bytes) from the current address. It helps to enable programs to be written which can run anywhere in memory (i.e. position independent code).

Relative Co-Ordinates

A graphics co-ordinate system in which the position of the next point is given as a displacement from the current point. Generally, relative co-ordinates are not as easy to use as absolute co-ordinates. They are found mostly on the simpler home computers, but some of the better machines give a choice of either relative or absolute.

Relocatable Code

A form of machine code program which can be adjusted to run at any location in memory by the use of a special program called a relocator, which corrects any absolute addresses used in the program to those required for where it is to run.

Reset

If a computer is reset it is taken back to its start-up state. This generally means that any data in RAM will be lost. To reset the MS-DOS computers the "Alt", "Ctrl", and "Del" keys must all be pressed simultaneously. It is almost impossible to accidentally press this combination of keys. Many computers (including a lot of MS-DOS machines) have a reset button. This is sometimes tucked away in an inaccessible place where it is not likely to be pressed accidentally. You would normally only need to reset a computer when it has crashed and has hung-up in a state where it refuses to take any of the instructions normally used with the applications program it was running. Resetting some computers does not always have the desired effect. It is then necessary to resort to switching off the computer, waiting a few seconds, and then switching on again.

Resident

Usually used to describe a program which is held permanently in memory, and which is run usually by pressing a combination of keys, while another program is in memory and running (but suspended while the resident program is in operation). Resident programs are usually such things as diaries and calculators. Do not confuse resident programs with background programs such as clocks and alarms, which are also permanently in memory, but running, though the user will not be aware of them for most of the time.

Resolution

This generally refers to the screen resolution of a computer, and it is measured in terms of horizontal and vertical pixels. A pixel is simply a dot on the screen, and the display is built up from thousands of these. For example, in its highest resolution mode the Atari ST computer has a screen resolution of 640 by 400 pixels. The higher the resolution, the greater the detail that can be shown on graphics displays. If you encounter a screen resolution of something like 80 by 25, this will almost certainly be the text resolution (i.e. 80 columns of text characters by 25 lines of characters) and not the graphics resolution.

RGB

This stands for Red Green Blue, and is a standard for sending signals from a computer to a monitor where each of the primary colours has a separate wire controlling it. There are in fact two standards, logic level RGB, where each colour can be either on or off, limiting the display to eight colours, and analogue RGB, where the level of each colour is continuously variable, allowing shaded colours.

RGBI

A system for sending signals from a computer to a monitor which is similar to logic level RGB, but where there is an extra wire allowing each colour to be either half-intensity or full-intensity, increasing the range of colours which can be displayed.

RISC

An acronym for Reduced Instruction Set Chip. The idea of these is that, instead of a large set of complex instructions, this type of microprocessor has only a small set of simple instructions, the instructions which most microprocessors spend most of their time doing anyway. By reducing the time taken to decode the instructions in a program, execution speed is increased. When necessary, the complex instructions can be made up by combinations of the simple ones. This type of chip is currently growing in popularity.

RS232C

This is the most common form of serial interface used in computing, and few computer serial interfaces are of a different type. Serial interfaces generally operate well over reasonably long distances, and need relatively few connecting wires. The transfer of data is often comparatively slow, but as many computer peripherals are even slower, this is often of no importance in practice! Some computers (such as the BBC model B etc.) are fitted with an RS423 serial interface. This is largely RS232C compatible, and there are not usually any problems in using a computer of this type with equipment fitted with an RS232C interface.

Scanner

A scanner could be regarded as the opposite of a printer or plotter. A drawing or photograph is placed in the unit, and then this is scanned by a photo-electric device. With suitable software, information from the scanner is used to build up the picture in a form that can be used with a graphics application program such as GEM Paint. Some scanners are complete units, but some low cost types are just the photo-electric part of the system. This second type are designed to operate in conjunction with a particular printer or plotter which scans the photo-cell over the picture.

Sector

Data is stored on floppy discs in a number of concentric tracks (usually forty or eighty on each side of a disc). Each track is sub-divided into sectors, and there are usually eight or nine of these per track. This compartmentalisation of a disc helps the operating system to rapidly access any desired data stored on the disc.

Sequential File

The simplest form of computer file, in which the records can only be read in sequence, starting from the beginning. In processing a sequential file, it is normal to read all the file into memory, and, if changes are made, to subsequently send the entire file to disc, discarding the previous version. In BASIC programming, the records would normally be read into arrays. Sequential files are economic of disc space, as no space is wasted padding records to a fixed length.

Software

Another name for programs, and programs of any description come under this category. In fact data for programs (such as libraries of pictures for graphics programs) would also qualify as software.

Source Code

In assembly language and compiled languages, the source code is the text file which is written by the programmer and read by the assembler/compiler to produce the object code. It is sometimes used to describe the written form of a program in an interpreted language such as BASIC, but this use is not strictly correct.

Spooler
This is usually a piece of software which enables the computer to print out a file while carrying on with another task as well. It is sometimes applied to a printer buffer, which is a device that includes a large amount of RAM. This enables a file to be loaded into the RAM, and then printed out from there, leaving the computer completely free to get on with other tasks.

Spreadsheet
A general-purpose type of mathematical program, where numeric data can be entered in rows and columns of "cells", and other cells can contain formulae, or mathematical functions containing references to some of the data stored in the spreadsheet. The results of evaluating the formulae are displayed in the cells containing them. For example, at the bottom of a column of figures, you could have a formula to add the figures in the columns together, displaying the sum. If some of the data contained in the spreadsheet is altered, all the formulae can be recalculated (automatically or on demand), showing the effect of the changes. These programs are therefore much used in financial planning, and have been termed "what if" programs.

Stack
A stack is an area of memory reserved for use by the computer CPU in executing a program. It is also used by the CPU to 'remember its place' in a program when called upon to service an interrupt. The main feature of the stack is that it is organised on a 'last in – first out' basis. Some MPUs allow multiple stacks so that, for instance, one can be used by the operating system and one by a high-level language.

System Disc
The system disc is the one which contains the operating system, and which is used at switch-on when booting the operating system into the computer.

Thermal Printer
A thermal printer is similar to a dot-matrix printer, but instead of pins in the head it has small heating elements. These either make marks on special thermal paper, or use a thermal ribbon which carries a film of ink which is melted onto plain paper by the printhead. Some thermal printers can use both systems. Thermal printers are usually inexpensive, frequently battery powered and portable, and give a quality of output ranging from till-roll abysmal to quite acceptable. They cannot produce carbon copies. A big advantage for some purposes is that they are very quiet, being matched in this only by the ink-jet printers which are substantially more expensive.

Toggle
Many programs use keys to "toggle" them between two operating modes. For instance, the word processor I am using to write this piece operates in the "insert" mode normally, but can be toggled to the "overwrite" mode by operating the "Ins" key. Operating the "Ins" key again takes the program back to the "insert" mode, operating it again takes the program into the "overwrite" mode once more, and so on. In other words, each time the key is operated the program is changed, or "toggled" to its alternative operating mode.

Track
Data is stored on a disc in a number of tracks around the disc. It is not like a gramophone record where there is one spiralling track on each side of the disc. A floppy disc has a number of concentric tracks, normally forty or eighty per side.

Transputer
This is a proprietary name for a particular family of microprocessor-type devices. The main feature of these is that they are designed so that a number of them can be used together in parallel processing applications, allowing very powerful computers to be built up. They can also be used singly. They are RISC type chips.

Turbo
This is a term which, in computing, is usually applied to an IBM compatible computer which operates at a higher clock speed than the original IBM machine. For example, a lot of PC "clones" operate at 8MHz, 10MHz, or even more, whereas the original PC has a clock speed of 4.77MHz. The higher clock speeds mean that these "turbo" computers carry out most tasks proportionately faster (some tasks, such as disc accesses, are not necessarily any faster). Most "turbo" computers have the ability to switch down to the standard clock frequency if desired. This facility is mainly included to avoid problems with some copy protected programs that refuse to run properly with the higher clock frequencies.

Turtle
The turtle is a feature of the LOGO computer language. The turtle can be either a robotic device which moves around on a sheet of paper on the floor, drawing lines by means of a pen (called a 'floor turtle') or it can be a symbol on the screen (usually a triangular pointer, but on some Atari computers it is actually a turtle shape, complete with cutesie feet!) which moves around leaving lines behind it. The turtle moves in response to commands such as FORWARD 50, RIGHT 90, BACKWARD 100 which move it specific distances and turn it through specific angles. Drawing can be stopped and started

with PENUP and PENDOWN. This type of graphics
has subsequently been incorporated in other languages (notably in versions of BASIC and FORTH) and
is now called Turtle Graphics.

User Friendly
A somewhat over-used phrase which supposedly
means that a piece of software (or possibly hardware) is easy to use, even for someone with little
knowledge of computing. Software which is totally
crash-proof and provides unambiguous instructions
whenever a command is required (preferably with
menu selection of commands) would be very user
friendly. A program which responds only to the
right combination of obscure letter codes would be
very user unfriendly. A point which is often overlooked is that user friendly programs, although easy
to use initially, may be rather slow going once you
have mastered them. Ideally a complex program
should offer user friendly control, with short cuts
available for experienced users.

Utilities
A term which describes programs that provide useful
but limited functions, and do not really qualify as
applications software. As an example, a program to
recover a deleted file from a disc would be a typical
utility.

WIMP
This is an acronym for Window Icon Mouse Pointer,
and describes the type of graphical front end environment popularised by the Apple Macintosh computer,
and since copied by such products as DR GEM and
Microsoft WINDOWS et al.

Winchester Disc
This is a type of hard disc, but hard discs are generally just referred to as such these days, or the alternative
name of "fixed disc" is used.

Word Processor
This very popular type of program (which naturally
is being used to write this book) allows text to be
entered from the keyboard, altered, edited, added to,
deleted, formatted and finally printed out. Additional
facilities allow text to be stored on disc, and allow
documents to be merged or split into parts. The
best word processors will also provide a thesaurus and
a spelling checker, and may allow you to work on
more than one document at once, copying text
between them.

Word-Wrap
Word-wrap (also known as wrap-around) is a word
processing term. It simply means that when the end
of a line is reached, the current word is transferred to
the beginning of the next line. This avoids having
words split between two lines. Unlike a typewriter,
when using a word processor it is not necessary to
put in carriage returns at the end of each line. The
carriage returns are effectively added for you by the
automatic word wrapping. This is a standard word
processor feature, and you are unlikely to find one
which does not incorporate it.

Write-Protect
Usually this means place a write-protect tab on a
floppy disc so that it is impossible to write data to
it. It can still be read of course. It is normal to fix
write-protect tabs onto program discs so that there
is no risk of accidentally over-writing and damaging
the program. Data discs which hold important data
should be treated in the same way. In fact it is more
important to use write-protect tabs on these as
inadvertent over-writing of files is more easily done
with data discs. Some systems support software
write-protect schemes.

XORing
See BITWISE.

Chapter 8

MIDI TECHNICALITIES

MIDI is an acronym for "Musical Instruments Digital Interface". Computers are now very much part of the electronic music world, and really seem to be a vital part of it these days. Few computers have a MIDI interface as standard (they are present on the Atari ST series and a few others), but they are available as add-ons for all the popular microcomputers. MIDI is a form of serial interface, and it is very similar to the standard RS232C and RS423 computer serial interfaces. The RS232C serial system has various word formats, with from 5 to 8 data bits, one or two stop bits, and sometimes a form of error detection known as parity checking is implemented. This system of error detection involves the transmission of extra bits on some bytes. Fortunately, MIDI is properly standardised, and it only ues a word format of one start bit, eight data bits, one stop bit, and no parity. This word format can be accommodated by all the serial interface chips I have encountered, and MIDI hardware does not require any non-standard components.

A lot of problems are experienced by users of RS232C equipment due to difficulties with the handshake lines. These enable a receiving device to instruct the sending equipment to temporarily halt the flow of data in the event that data is received at a higher rate than it can be processed. There is no risk of any similar problems with MIDI interfacing as handshaking is not used. At least, handshaking of the hardware variety is not used. Some equipment uses system exclusive messages where a two-way dialogue takes place so that the flow of data can be regulated, and any errors can be corrected. This system can work very well, and the lack of hardware handshaking is not a major drawback.

Some serial systems are "synchronous", which means that they use an extra connecting cable to carry some form of synchronisation signal. MIDI is a form of "asynchronous" serial interface, which means that the timing signals are sent on the same line as the data. In fact the only synchronisation signal is the start bit at the beginning of each byte. This indicates the commencement of a byte of data, and that the voltage on the connecting lead must be tested at regular intervals thereafter until a full byte of data has been received. It does not ensure that the transmitting and sending devices are properly synchronised while each byte of data is sent. This is achieved by sending/receiving data at a standard rate, with (usually) quartz crystal controlled oscillators (as used in quartz watches) to ensure excellent accuracy at both ends of the link.

The standard MIDI "baud" rate is 31250 baud, or 31.25 kilobaud if you prefer. This simply means that data is transmitted at a rate of 31250 bits per second (assuming a continuous flow of data). This is not a standard RS232C baud rate, and might seem to be an unusual choice. Originally the baud rate was 19200 baud, which is the highest standard baud rate for RS232C interfaces. However, this was deemed to be too slow, and in the final MIDI specification it was increased to 31250 baud. This is convenient from the hardware point of view, as it is well within the capabilities of most serial interface chips. Also, 31250 multiplied by 32 equals 1000000, and this fact enables the baud rate of MIDI interfaces to be controlled using "off the shelf" crystals intended for communications applications and microprocessor circuits.

The Hardware
RS232C and RS423 interfaces use different voltages to represent logic 0 and logic 1 levels, but MIDI is different in that it uses a 5 milliamp current loop. In other words, the current is switched on to indicate one logic level, and switched off to represent the other logic state. This is done due to the use of opto-isolators at each input, which keep items of equipment in the system electrically isolated from one another. This eliminates the risk of damage occurring when two or more items of equipment are connected together, due to their chassis being at different voltages. It also helps to reduce the risk of "hum" loops being produced when a number of instruments and other equipment are connected together. Finally, it also helps to avoid having electrical noise coupled from a computer into the audio stages of an instrument. If there is one thing computers do better than space invaders or number crunching it is generating electrical noise! Refer to the relevant section of Chapter 2 for MIDI port connection details.

MIDI Codes
All MIDI instructions have a header byte that consists of two 4 bit sections (or "nibbles" as they are sometimes called). The most significant nibble indicates the nature of the instruction (note on, note off, or whatever). The least significant nibble is the channel number in most messages, but no channel number is required for any form of system message. With system messages the most significant nibble is the system message code, and the least significant nibble defines the precise type of system message (MIDI clock, reset, etc.). In terms of the total decimal value in a header byte, it is just a matter of taking the values of the two nibbles and adding them together. For instance, an instruction nibble of 128 and a channel value of 12 would be sent as a byte having a total value of 140. With MIDI it is often

easier to work with hexadecimal numbers, as each nibble represents one digit of a hexadecimal number.

The most significant bit of header bytes is always set to 1, but this bit of data bytes is always 0. It is for this reason that MIDI data bytes only cover a 0 to 127 range, and not the full 0 to 255 span afforded by 8 bit operation. The point of arranging things this way is that it enables receiving equipment to sort out MIDI messages from amongst MIDI data. Although this might appear to be unnecessary with one MIDI message being fully transmitted before the next one is commenced, things do not always happen in this way. It is obviously necessary for MIDI clock messages to be sent at strictly regular intervals, without them being delayed too long while a message in progress is completed. The MIDI specification therefore allows for clock messages to be mixed into other messages. Complete bytes must always be sent, and a byte must not be aborted so that a clock message can be sent. It is still possible to have something like a note on message and the note value sent, followed by a MIDI clock message, and then the velocity data byte of the note on message! As the most significant bit of the clock message will be set to 1, the receiving equipment can recognise it as such and will not mistake it for the velocity data byte.

Note On/Off

The note on nibble is 1001 in binary, which is equivalent to 144 in decimal. From here onwards, values will be provided in binary, followed by the decimal equivalent shown in brackets. The least significant nibble is the channel number, which is from 0000 (0) to 1111 (15). As MIDI channels are normally numbered from 1 to 16, this means that the value used in a MIDI channel message to select the desired channel is actually one less than the MIDI channel number. In other words a value of 0 selects channel 1, a value of 1 selects channel 2, and so on. The note on message is followed by two data bytes, which are the note number and the velocity value.

Note off messages have 1000 (128) as the most significant nibble, and the channel number as the least significant nibble. The header byte is followed by two data bytes, which are again the note number and velocity value. A note on message having a velocity value of 0 can be used as an alternative form of note off message.

Key Pressure

Overall key pressure (sometimes called "channel" pressure) has the instruction nibble 1101 (208) and is followed by a single data byte. Polyphonic key pressure has 1010 (160) as the instruction nibble, and is followed by two data bytes. These are the note value first, and the pressure value second. For both types of message the least significant nibble of the header byte contains the channel number.

Control Change Etc.

The control change header byte has 1011 (176) as the most significant nibble in the header byte, while the least significant nibble is the channel number value. The header is followed by two data bytes, which are the control number followed by its new value. Controls from 0 to 31 are paired with controls from 32 to 63 (respectively), and these operate as high resolution continuous controls. Each pair of seven bit numbers are combined to give a single 14 bit value. The lower numbered controller always provides the most significant bits, with the higher numbered control providing the seven least significant bits. In terms of decimal numbers, the range available is from 0 to 16383. Note that it is quite acceptable to only change one or other of the controls in a pair, and a change to one does not necessitate a change to the other.

Not all equipment actually uses the high resolution capability of the MIDI continuous controls, and most equipment only uses a resolution of seven bits or less. For 7 bit resolution it is the most significant nibble (lower control number) that is utilised, and the least significant one that is ignored. For less than seven bit resolution the least significant bit or bits are left at zero, while the most significant bits are utilised.

Control numbers from 64 to 95 are used for switch type controls. Only control values of 0 (off) and 127 (on) are valid with these, and other control values will be ignored. Control numbers from 96 to 121 are, as yet, unassigned. These are available for future expansion, and may be assigned specific functions in the future.

The remaining control numbers (122 to 127) are used for mode changes and similar functions. These have a value of 0 for the control value byte, apart from controls 122 (local on/off) and 126 (mono on). Local control is a standard on/off switch type control, and is 127 to activate the keyboard (or whatever), and 0 to switch it off. When mono mode is switched on, the control value selects the number of voices to be set to mono mode (a value of 0 sets all the instrument's voices to mono mode). The MIDI specification only calls for mono mode channels to be contiguous, but some instruments have special modes which allow them to be assigned to any desired channels.

Pitch Wheel

The pitch wheel header byte has 1110 (224) as its most significant nibble, and the channel number value as the least significant nibble. Two data bytes are used, and the two seven bit values these contain are combined to give a 14 bit pitch wheel value. The least significant byte is the one sent first. A value of 10000000000000 (8192) represents zero pitch change. If less than the full 14 bit resolution is implemented some of the least significant bits are ignored by a receiving device, and always set at zero by a transmitting device.

Program Change

The program change code nibble is 1100 (192). The least significant nibble of the header byte is the channel number value. The header is followed by a single data byte, which is the number of the new program for that channel. The value in the data byte is from 0 to 127, but some manufacturers number programs differently. Where this is the case, equipment manuals often have a conversion chart to make things easier.

Table 1 provides a summary of the channel messages for quick reference purposes. The channel mode messages require some further amplification, and this is provided in Table 2.

Table 1

Header	Function	Data
1000 (128)	Note Off	Note Value/Velocity Value
1001 (144)	Note On	Note Value/Velocity Value
1010 (160)	Poly Key Pressure	Note Value/Pressure Value
1011 (176)	Control Change	Control Number/Value
1100 (192)	Program Change	New Program Number
1101 (208)	Overall Pressure	Pressure Value
1110 (224)	Pitch Wheel	l.s.b./m.s.b.

Table 2

Control No.	Function	Data
122	Local Control	0 = off, 127 = on
123	All Notes Off	0
124	Omni Mode Off	0
125	Omni Mode On	0
126	Mono Mode On	Number Of Channels (0 = All Channels Set To Mono Mode)
127	Poly Mode On	0

System Messages

These all have 1111 (240) as the most significant nibble in the header byte. No channel numbers are used, as these messages are sent to the whole system. This leaves the least significant nibble free to indicate the type of system message. Table 3 gives a full list of these messages, but note that some of the sixteen available codes are as yet undefined. Many of them do not require data bytes, and are just single byte messages.

The values shown in brackets are the decimal equivalents for the binary nibbles. These must be boosted by 240 to give the total decimal value for each header byte (e.g. the value sent for a clock signal is 240 + 8 = 248). The system exclusive message is followed by a data byte which gives the manufacturer's identification code, and then as many data bytes as required follow on from this. The "end system exclusive" message marks the end of a system exclusive message.

Table 3

Nibble Code	Function	Data
0000 (0)	System Exclusive	ID/As Required
0001 (1)	Undefined	
0010 (2)	Song Position Pointer	l.s.b./m.s.b.
0011 (3)	Song Select	Song Number
0100 (4)	Undefined	
0101 (5)	Undefined	
0110 (6)	Tune Request	None
0111 (7)	End System Exclusive	None
1000 (8)	Clock Signal	None
1001 (9)	Undefined	
1010 (10)	Start	None
1011 (11)	Continue	None
1100 (12)	Stop	None
1101 (13)	Undefined	
1110 (14)	Active Sensing	None
1111 (15)	System Reset	None

Table 4 provides a list of manufacturer's identification numbers. The sample dump standard is a "system exclusive common" message, which can be used by any MIDI equipment producer.

Table 4

Manufacturer	Number (decimal)
SC1	1
Big Briar	2
Octave	3
Moog	4
Passport Designs	5
Lexicon	6
Ensonique	15
Oberheim	16
Bon Tempi	32
SIEL	33
Kawai	64
Roland	65
Korg	66
Yamaha	67
Casio	68
Sample Dump Standard	126

Appendix A

ASCII TABLE

Decimal	Hex	Binary	Character	Decimal	Hex	Binary	Character
0	00	0000000	NUL	54	36	0110	6
1	01	0001	SOH	55	37	0111	7
2	02	0010	STX	56	38	1000	8
3	03	0011	ETX	57	39	1001	9
4	04	0100	EOT	58	3A	1010	:
5	05	0101	ENQ	59	3B	1011	;
6	06	0110	ACK	60	3C	1100	<
7	07	0111	BEL	61	3D	1101	=
8	08	1000	BS	62	3E	1110	>
9	09	1001	HT	63	3F	1111	?
10	0A	1010	LF	64	40	1000000	@
11	0B	1011	VT	65	41	0001	A
12	0C	1100	FF	66	42	0010	B
13	0D	1101	CR	67	43	0011	C
14	0E	1110	SO	68	44	0100	D
15	0F	1111	SI	69	45	0101	E
16	10	0010000	DLE	70	46	0110	F
17	11	0001	DC1	71	47	0111	G
18	12	0010	DC2	72	48	1000	H
19	13	0011	DC3	73	49	1001	I
20	14	0100	DC4	74	4A	1010	J
21	15	0101	NAK	75	4B	1011	K
22	16	0110	SYN	76	4C	1100	L
23	17	0111	ETB	77	4D	1101	M
24	18	1000	CAN	78	4E	1110	N
25	19	1001	EM	79	4F	1111	O
26	1A	1010	SUB	80	50	1010000	P
27	1B	1011	ESC	81	51	0001	Q
28	1C	1100	FS	82	52	0010	R
29	1D	1101	GS	83	53	0011	S
30	1E	1110	RS	84	54	0100	T
31	1F	1111	US	85	55	0101	U
32	20	0100000	[SPACE]	86	56	0110	V
33	21	0001	!	87	57	0111	W
34	22	0010	"	88	58	1000	X
35	23	0011	#	89	59	1001	Y
36	24	0100	$	90	5A	1010	Z
37	25	0101	%	91	5B	1011	[
38	26	0110	&	92	5C	1100	\
39	27	0111	'	93	5D	1101	]
40	28	1000	(	94	5E	1110	^
41	29	1001	)	95	5F	1111	←
42	2A	1010	*	96	60	1100000	`
43	2B	1011	+	97	61	0001	a
44	2C	1100	,	98	62	0010	b
45	2D	1101	—	99	63	0011	c
46	2E	1110	.	100	64	0100	d
47	2F	1111	/	101	65	0101	e
48	30	0110000	0	102	66	0110	f
49	31	0001	1	103	67	0111	g
50	32	0010	2	104	68	1000	h
51	33	0011	3	105	69	1001	i
52	34	0100	4	106	6A	1010	j
53	35	0101	5	107	6B	1011	k

Decimal	Hex	Binary	Character		Decimal	Hex	Binary	Character
108	6C	1100	l		118	76	0110	v
109	6D	1101	m		119	77	0111	w
110	6E	1110	n		120	78	1000	x
111	6F	1111	o		121	79	1001	y
112	70	1110000	p		122	7A	1010	z
113	71	0001	q		123	7B	1011	{
114	72	0010	r		124	7C	1100		
115	73	0011	s		125	7D	1101	}
116	74	0100	t		126	7E	1110	~
117	75	0101	u		127	7F	1111	DEL

EPSON STANDARD PRINTER CONTROLS

The EPSON standard printer control sequences (ESC-P) are used by many other manufacturers, and are the accepted industry standard. Only the basic control sequences are given here. For the full syntax, number of extra bytes required, etc. refer to your printer manual or to Babani book number BP181 "Getting the Most from your Printer".

No one printer utilises all the codes given here. Again, you should consult your printer manual to find which codes are functional on your machine. Some printers, while generally conforming to the codes given here, may use different codes for some particular functions, or may implement some functions in a different or non-standard way. Actual line spacings may be different from those given below, especially in portable printers and those with more than 9 print pins.

Code Sequence	Function
	TYPE STYLES
SO	Enlarged (one line only)
ESC SO	Same as SO
DC4	Cancel the above
ESC W	Set/cancel enlarged
SI	Condensed
ESC SI	Same as SI
DC2	Cancel condensed
ESC E	Set emphasised
ESC F	Cancel emphasised
ESC G	Set double strike
ESC H	Cancel double strike
ESC 4	Set italic
ESC 5	Cancel italic
ESC M	Set 12-pitch
ESC g	Set 15-pitch
ESC P	Cancel 12/15 pitch
ESC −	Set/cancel underline
ESC S	Set super/subscript
ESC T	Cancel super/subscript
ESC !	Set any combination of styles
ESC p	Set/cancel proportional spacing
ESC x	Set/cancel letter quality
ESC k	Select character style
	GRAPHICS MODES (DOT GRAPHICS)
ESC K	Normal density bit image
ESC L	Dual density bit image
ESC Y	Fast dual density bit image
ESC Z	Quad density bit image
ESC ^	Nine pin bit image
ESC ?	Reassign ESC K, L, Y, Z
ESC *	Select any bit image mode

Code Sequence	Function
	REDEFINABLE CHARACTERS
ESC :	Copy ROM characters into RAM
ESC &	Define downloadable character(s)
ESC %	Select ROM/RAM characters
ESC 6	Set codes 128−159 as printable
ESC 7	Set codes 128−159 as controls
ESC I	Set unused codes as printable
ESC m	Set codes 128−159 as graphics
	LINE SPACING
ESC 0	Set line spacing to $1/8''$
ESC 1	Set line spacing to $7/72''$
ESC 2	Set line spacing to $1/6''$
ESC 3	Set line spacing to $n/216''$
ESC A	Set line spacing to $n/72''$
	CHARACTER SPACING/ JUSTIFICATION
ESC sp	Set character spacing
ESC $	Set absolute dot position
ESC \	Set relative dot position
ESC a	Set justification mode
	TABLES AND FORMS
ESC C	Set page length
ESC N	Set auto perforation skip
ESC O	Cancel perforation skip
VT	Execute vertical tab
ESC B	Set vertical tabs
ESC /	Set VFU channel
ESC b	Set VFU positions
ESC l	Set left margin
ESC Q	Set right margin
HT	Execute horizontal tab
ESC D	Set horizontal tabs
ESC e	Set horizontal/vertical tab spacing
ESC f	Set skip positions
	PRINTER OPERATING COMMANDS
CR	Carriage return
LF	Line feed
FF	Form feed
BS	Backspace
ESC i	Incremental print mode
ESC J	$n/216''$ line feed
ESC j	$n/216''$ reverse feed
	OTHERS
ESC t	Select code table
ESC R	Select international character set
CAN	Clear print buffer
DEL	Delete last character
DC1	Enable printer

Code Sequence	Function	Code Sequence	Function
DC3	Disable printer	ESC 8	Disable paper-end detector
ESC V	Select auto character repeat	ESC 9	Enable paper-end detector
ESC #	Cancel MSB control	ESC U	Select unidirectional print
ESC >	Force MSB to 1	ESC <	Unidirectional print (one line)
ESC =	Force MSB to 0	ESC s	Select quiet (half-speed print)
BEL	Sound bell/beeper	ESC r	Select print colour
ESC @	Initialise printer	ESC EM	Operate sheet feeder

ABBREVIATIONS

ALT
Alternate. A key to be found on many computer keyboards. It is a form of shift key and does not generate a printable character.

ANSI
The American National Standards Institute. A body which lays down various standards, including some computer standards (which are not necessarily adhered to by manufacturers).

ASCII
American Standard Code for Information Interchange. ASCII is the standard form of binary coding for text characters, although there are some computers which use alternatives (notably the Sinclair Spectrum series).

ASM
This is a popular abbreviation for an "assembler".

BBS
Bulletin Board System. A system that can be accessed using a modem and computer to download programs, articles, or whatever, amongst other things.

CAD
Computer Aided Drawing (or Drafting). A program or computer system for producing accurate technical drawings. CAD can also stand for "computer aided design". In this context it usually means a program that mathematically models something (electronic circuits, wear on engine parts, etc.). It effectively enables something to be tested without actually having to make it.

CAE
Computer Aided Education. Any program or computer system which is intended for educational use.

CAM
Computer Aided Manufacture. A program or computer system that aids the manufacture of something (computerised cutting equipment in the textile industry for example).

CGA
Colour Graphics Adaptor. The CGA card has been the most popular colour graphics board for the IBM PC and compatibles, although it seems likely to be overtaken by EGA and VGA boards in the near future. Its two graphics modes are 640 x 200 in 2 colours and 320 x 200 in 4 colours.

CISC
Comprehensive Instruction Set Computer. The normal type of microprocessor in other words (not a RISC type).

CMOS
Complementary Metal Oxide Semiconductor. This is a general type of chip, and it refers to a particular method of manufacture. Most types of computer chip are available in CMOS forms, and the main advantage of this technology is that it provides very low power consumption.

CP/M
Control Program for Microcomputers. This is the standard operating system for 8 bit (Z80 or 8080 based) computers.

CPI
Characters Per Inch. This is a printer term, and is merely the number of characters in a one inch line of text.

CPS
Characters Per Second. A printer term used as a measure of a printer's speed. It is the number of characters printed per second, and often needs to be taken with the proverbial "pinch of salt".

CPU
Central Processing Unit. Another name for a microprocessor.

CR
Carriage Return. Takes the print head of a printer back to the beginning of a line (and in practice is usually accompanied by a linefeed which winds the paper up to the next line).

DD
Disc Drive (usually applied to floppy rather than hard discs).

DMP
Dot Matrix Printer.

DOS
Disc Operating System. Simply an operating system that is loaded from disc.

DPI
Dot Per Inch. A printer term — the more dots per inch the better the print quality is likely to be.

DRAM

Dynamic Random Access Memory. A type of RAM chip (the type used in most computers).

DSDD

Double Sided Double Density. A disc format — uses both sides of the disc with double the standard amount of data per track.

DSSD

Double Sided Single Density. A disc format — uses both sides of the disc with the standard amount of data per track.

DTP

Desk Top Publishing. A computer system that enables documents (newsletters, magazines, books, reports, advertising sheets, etc.) to be prepared. It differs from a word processor in that a wide variety of lettering styles, fonts, and sizes are available, and in most cases graphics can also be incorporated in the document.

EEPROM

Electronically Programmable Read Only Memory. An EEPROM device differs from an EPROM type in that it can be electronically erased.

EGA

Enhanced Graphics Adaptor. This is a video adaptor card for IBM PCs and most compatibles. Its main mode provides 640 × 350 resolution in 16 colours.

EMS

A standard for extended memory boards for IBM PCs and compatibles (enables them to go beyond the normal 640k limit, but only operates with software written to support this standard).

EPROM

Erasable Programmable Read Only Memory. This type of memory circuit differs from ROM in that it is not programmed at the manufacturing stage. Instead it is programmed using a special programmer (which is often an add-on device for a computer rather than a stand-alone unit). EPROM can be erased using ultra-violet light, and then reprogrammed.

ESC

Escape. A key that is found on most computer keyboards. Its function depends on the particular computer in use, and in most cases on the software it is running.

FDD

Floppy Disc Drive.

FF

Form Feed. If a printer is sent a form feed it advances the paper to the end of the page.

HD

Hard Disc.

HPGL

Hewlett Packard Graphics Language. This is the graphics language used for Hewlett Packard plotters, and emulations of it are used by several other plotter manufacturers. Most software that has plotter support can be used with HPGL or HPGL emulation plotters.

I/O

Input/Output. A term that generally refers to the ports of a computer, but which can be applied to any form of input and output (reading and writing to disc for instance).

IC

Integrated Circuit. The components on which computers are based — a microprocessor is a type of integrated circuit. (If you look inside a computer, the black plastic components having two rows of pins are the integrated circuits [some ICs these days have different types of case, including large square ones with pins on all four sides] .)

K

Kilobyte (1024 bytes).

KB

Kilobyte.

LAN

Local Area Network. A setup which has two or more computers connected together to effectively operate as a single system.

LC

Lower Case (i.e. small letters, not capitals).

LF

Linefeed. If a printer is sent a linefeed it advances the paper by one line (but does not move to the beginning of the line which requires a carriage return).

LQ

Letter Quality. A printer term which applies to the quality of the printed text. LQ is high quality text, comparable to that provided by a good quality typewriter.

M

Megabyte (1048576 bytes).

MB

Megabyte.

Micro

Microcomputer or Microprocessor. These days the term "micro" is more usually applied to a microcomputer than to a microprocessor.

MIDI

Musical Instruments Digital Interface. This is a form of serial interface that enables a computer to operate in conjunction with a suitably equipped electronic musical instrument. It is not compatible with the standard RS232C computer serial interface.

MODEM

Modulator – Demodulator. A device which enables computer systems to communicate via the telephone system.

MOS

Maching Operating System or Metal Oxide Silicon. The first is a computer operating system such as MS-DOS or CP/M, and the second is a manufacturing process for integrated circuits (many computer ICs are of the MOS variety).

MPU

Microprocessor Unit. This is just another term for a microprocessor.

MS-DOS

Microsoft Disc Operating System. The standard operating system for IBM PC compatible computers, and a few other machines.

NLQ

Near Letter Quality. Most dot matrix printers provide rather mediocre print quality at their highest printing speed. Most have near letter quality mode which provides a much higher print quality by using a double-pass system (but the print speed is usually much lower).

OS

Operating System (MS-DOS, CP/M, etc.).

PC

Personal Computer. Any microcomputer could be called a personal computer, but these days it generally refers to a business micro. In fact it is most often applied to IBM compatible computers.

PC-DOS

Personal Computer Disc Operating System. The operating system used on the IBM PCs (compatibles use the very similar MS-DOS).

PD

Public Domain. In a computer context this applies to software which is free. What you pay for when you buy PD software is merely the cost of the disc, duplication fees, etc. PD is different to "shareware" software in that the latter is free to try out, but if you go on using it the author requires a registration fee.

QWERTY

This does not stand for anything. It is the first six letters on the top (letters) row of a typewriter style keyboard. A QWERTY keyboard is therefore just an ordinary computer keyboard.

RAM

Random Access Memory. This is memory which the computer can use to store data and read it back again.

RISC

Reduced Instruction Set Computer. A computer based on a microprocessor that has a relatively small number of instructions, but each one can be performed very rapidly.

ROM

Read Only Memory. A form of memory which is programmed at the manufacturing stage. Thus the computer can only read ROM, it can not alter its contents.

SSDD

Single Sided Double Density. A disc format – only uses one side of the disc but places twice the normal amount of data on each track.

SSSD

Single Sided Single Density. A disc format – only uses one side of the disc and places the standard amount of data in each track.

UART

Universal Asynchronous Receiver/Transmitter. This is a type of serial interface integrated circuit. It is a general purpose type which is not intended for operation with one particular family of microprocessor. In fact they are usable with non-microprocessor based systems as well.

UC

Upper Case (i.e. capital letters).

VDI

Visual Display Interface. Less well known alternative to VDU.

VDU

Visual Display Unit. This usually refers to a terminal unit (i.e. a keyboard and monitor plus supporting electronics), which is usually one of many terminals connected to a mini or mainframe computer.

VGA

Video Graphics Array. This is the video circuit in the IBM PS/2 series of computers. Add-on VGA cards for the IBM PC and most compatibles are also available. It includes all the standard IBM PC graphics standards as well as some new ones (including a 640 x 480 16 colour mode, and a 320 x 200 256 colour mode).

WIMP

Windows – Icons – Mouse – Pointer. A graphics based computer environment which makes use of a mouse to manipulate things via on-screen windows, pointer, and icons (as with GEM for example).

WP

Word Processor.

WYSIWYG

What You See Is What You Get. A term mostly used with word processors where the on-screen text looks (more or less) like the printed out version.

Appendix D

SUPPORT CHIPS

Designing the hardware for a computer is probably not as difficult as most computer users would imagine. The microprocessor manufacturers also produce what, in general, is a useful range of support chips, and these greatly ease the problem of computer hardware design. At one time most computers consisted of a microprocessor, memory chips, some standard peripheral chips, a few general purpose logic devices, and pieces of hardware such as the drives and keyboard. In modern computers the standard peripheral chips are perhaps less in evidence, and there has been a marked trend towards custom chips which combine functions of several peripheral devices plus some general logic devices in one purpose made integrated circuit. Rightly or wrongly, this is generally thought to give better reliability, and provided the computer sells in suitably large numbers, it is certainly cheaper. Despite the trend towards custom chips, most computers still have some standard peripheral devices (the sound chip of the Atari ST computers for example, is the standard AY-3-8910 or equivalent, as found in several other machines).

This is a list of some common microprocessors and their standard support chips, plus a list of non-microprocessor specific devices. Note that a device which is intended specifically for one microprocessor is often usable with many other types, albeit with a certain amount of difficulty in most cases. Some microprocessors are (more or less) bus compatible with other microprocessors, and their peripheral chips are then largely interchangeable (the 6800 and 6502 series of microprocessors are a good example of this). Sometimes peripheral devices are used in a computer even though, on the face of it, they seem to be largely incompatible with the microprocessor used in the design. The Z80A based Amstrad CPC computers for example, use the 6845 video chip which is really intended for use with the 6800 series of microprocessors.

6502

6520	Parallel I/O interface
6522	Parallel I/O interface and twin 16 bit timers
6526	Parallel I/O interface and timers (Commodore)
6532	RAM – I/O – Timer combination
6541	Keyboard/display controller
6545	Display controller
6551	Serial I/O interface
6566	Video controller (Commodore)
6567	Video controller (Commodore)
6581	Sound generator (Commodore)

The standard devices are for operation up to 1MHz. Those having a "B" suffix can operate up to 1.5MHz, and those with a "C" suffix are suitable for use up to 2MHz. Where indicated, the devices are manufactured by Commodore Business Machines Ltd and are not in general use.

Z80

Z80PIO	Parallel I/O interface
Z80CTC	Timers
Z80DART	Dual serial I/O interface
Z80DMA	Direct memory access
Z80SIO	Serial I/O interface

The standard devices are suitable for clock frequencies of up to 2.5MHz. The "A" suffix chips (as used in many computers) are suitable for operation at frequencies up to 4MHz.

6800

6821	Parallel I/O interface
6828	Interrupt controller
6840	Timer/counter
6844	DMA controller
6846	ROM – I/O – Timer combination
6850	Asynchronous serial I/O interface
6852	Synchronous serial I/O interface
6871	Clock generator
6875	Clock generator

The standard devices are suitable for clock frequencies up to 1MHz. The "B" suffix devices can operate up to 1.5MHz, while the "C" suffix devices are suitable for use up to 2MHz.

8080

8155	RAM – I/O – Timer combination
8224	Clock generator
8228	Control/data bus demultiplexer
8250	Asynchronous serial I/O interface
8251	Universal serial I/O interface
8253	Timer (3 x 16 bit)
8255	Parallel I/O interface
8256	Multi-function serial I/O interface
8257	DMA controller
8259	Interrupt controller
8279	Keyboard/display interface

8080 series peripherals have good bus compatibility with the Z80 microprocessor, and are often used in Z80 based computers.

68000

68230	Parallel I/O and timer/counters
68450	DMA controller
68451	Memory manager
68661	Communications controller
68681	Serial I/O interface

The 68000 series of microprocessors can also be interfaced to 6800 peripheral chips.

8086

Uses 8080 series peripheral chips.

General Support Chips

76489	Three channel (plus noise) sound generator
AY-3-8910	Three channel (plus noise) sound generator, plus dual parallel I/O ports
AY-3-8912	As above but without the parallel ports
AY-3-1015	UART (universal asynchronous receiver/transmitter)
6402	UART (universal asynchronous receiver/transmitter)
ZN427E	Analogue to digital converter
ZN447E	Analogue to digital converter
ZN426E	Digital to analogue converter
ZN428E	Digital to analogue converter
446818	Real-time clock and CMOS RAM
58174	Real-time clock
58274	Real-time clock
SPO256	Speech Synthesiser
74C922	Keyboard decoder
74C923	Keyboard decoder
TMS9929A	Video controller

Appendix E

DECIMAL – BINARY – HEX

Decimal	Binary	Hexadecimal	Decimal	Binary	Hexadecimal
0	0	0	51	110011	33
1	1	1	52	110100	34
2	10	2	53	110101	35
3	11	3	54	110110	36
4	100	4	55	110111	37
5	101	5	56	111000	38
6	110	6	57	111001	39
7	111	7	58	111010	3A
8	1000	8	59	111011	3B
9	1001	9	60	111100	3C
10	1010	A	61	111101	3D
11	1011	B	62	111110	3E
12	1100	C	63	111111	3F
13	1101	D	64	1000000	40
14	1110	E	65	1000001	41
15	1111	F	66	1000010	42
16	10000	10	67	1000011	43
17	10001	11	68	1000100	44
18	10010	12	69	1000101	45
19	10011	13	70	1000110	46
20	10100	14	71	1000111	47
21	10101	15	72	1001000	48
22	10110	16	73	1001001	49
23	10111	17	74	1001010	5A
24	11000	18	75	1001011	5B
25	11001	19	76	1001100	5C
26	11010	1A	77	1001101	5D
27	11011	1B	78	1001110	5E
28	11100	1C	79	1001111	5F
29	11101	1D	80	1010000	60
30	11110	1E	81	1010001	61
31	11111	1F	82	1010010	62
32	100000	20	83	1010011	63
33	100001	21	84	1010100	64
34	100010	22	85	1010101	65
35	100011	23	86	1010110	66
36	100100	24	87	1010111	67
37	100101	25	88	1011000	68
38	100110	26	89	1011001	69
39	100111	27	90	1011010	6A
40	101000	28	91	1011011	6B
41	101001	29	92	1011100	6C
42	101010	2A	93	1011101	6D
43	101011	2B	94	1011110	6E
44	101100	2C	95	1011111	6F
45	101101	2D	96	1100000	70
46	101110	2E	97	1100001	71
47	101111	2F	98	1100010	72
48	110000	30	99	1100011	73
49	110001	31	100	1100100	74
50	110010	32			

THE STANDARD SYMBOLS FOR USE IN FLOW-CHARTS

Manual Operation

Input/Output

Process

Terminal/Interrupt

Preparation

Decision

Merge

Document

Display

Connector

Manual Input

Off Page

Communications Link

Index